The Cast-iron Canvasser

"Grand idea isn't he! Lor' bless you, I fairly love him."   page 7

BANJO PATERSON

A Children's Treasury

Illustrated by
DEE HUXLEY

Lansdowne
Sydney Auckland London New York

This book belongs to

WELDON-HARDIE
—GROUP OF COMPANIES—

Designed by Dawn Daly
Published by Lansdowne Press
a division of RPLA Pty Limited,
372 Eastern Valley Way, Chatswood, NSW, 2067
First published 1984
Reprinted 1987
Illustrations © Lansdowne 1984
Poems and prose by A. B. Paterson first published prior to 1 May, 1969
— Copyright Reserved — Proprietor, Retusa Pty Limited
Poems and prose by A. B. Paterson first published 1983 © Retusa Pty
Limited 1983
Produced in Australia by the Publisher
Typeset in Australia by Savage Type Pty Ltd, Brisbane
Printed by Toppan Printing Co. (Sing.) Ltd

National Library of Australia Cataloguing-in-Publication Data

Paterson, A. B. (Andrew Barton), 1864–1941.
A children's treasury.

ISBN 0 7018 1892 1.

1. Children's poetry, Australian.
I. Huxley, Dee. II. Title.

A821'.2

CONTENTS

Contents

The Cast-iron Canvasser

THE FIRM of Sloper and Dodge, book publishers and printers, was in great distress. These two enterprising individuals had worked up an enormous business in time payment books, which they sold all over Australia by means of canvassers. They had put a lot of money into the business — all they had, in fact. And now, just as everything was in thorough working order, the public had revolted against them. Their canvassers were ill-treated and molested by the country folk in all sorts of strange bush ways. One man was made drunk, and then a two-horse harrow was run over him; another was decoyed out into the desolate ranges on pretence of being shown a gold mine, and then his guide galloped away and left him to freeze all night in the bush. In mining localities, on the appearance of a canvasser, the inhabitants were called together by beating a camp oven lid with a pick, and the canvasser was given ten minutes to leave the town alive. If he disregarded the hint he would as likely as not fall accidentally down a disused shaft. The people of one district applied to their member of Parliament to have canvassers brought under the Noxious Animals Act and demanded that a reward should be offered for their scalps. Reports were constantly published in the country press about strange, gigantic birds that appeared at remote free selections, and frightened the inhabitants to death — these were Sloper and Dodge's sober and reliable agents, wearing the neat, close-fitting suits of tar and feathers with which their enthusiastic yokel admirers had presented them. In fact, it was too hot altogether for the canvassers, and they came in from north and west and south, crippled and disheartened, and handed in their resignations. To make matters worse, Sloper and Dodge had just got out a map of Australasia on a great scale, and if they couldn't sell it, ruin stared them in the face; and how could they sell it without canvassers!

The two members of the firm sat in their private office. Sloper was a long, sanctimonious individual, very religious and very bald — "beastly, awfully bald". Dodge was a little, fat American, with bristly black hair and beard, and quick, beady eyes. He was eternally smoking a reeking black pipe, and swallowing the smoke, and then puffing it out through his nose in great whiffs, like a locomotive on a steep grade.

Anybody walking into one of those whiffs incautiously was likely to get paralysed, the tobacco was so strong.

As the firm waited, Dodge puffed nervously at his pipe and filled the office with noxious fumes. The two partners were in a very anxious and expectant condition.

Just as things were at their very blackest, an event had happened which promised to relieve all their difficulties. An inventor, a genius, had come forward, who offered to supply the firm with a patent cast-iron canvasser, a figure which he said when wound up would walk about, talk by means of a phonograph, collect orders, and stand any amount of ill usage and wear and tear. If this could indeed be done, then they were saved. They had made an appointment with the genius to inspect his figure, but he was half an hour late, and the partners were steeped in gloom.

Just as they despaired of his appearing at all, a cab rattled up to the door, and Sloper and Dodge rushed unanimously to the window. A young man, very badly dressed, stepped out of the cab, holding over his shoulder what looked like the upper half of a man's body. In his dis-engaged hand he held a pair of human legs with boots and trousers on. Thus equipped he turned to the cabman to ask his fare, but the man with a yell of terror whipped up his horse, and disappeared at a hand gallop, and a woman who happened to be going by went howling down the street, saying that "Jack the Ripper" had come to town. The man bolted in at the door, and toiled up the dark stairs, tramping heavily under his hideous load, the legs and feet which he dragged after him making an unearthly clatter. He came in and put his burden down on the sofa.

"There you are, gents," he said. "There's your canvasser."

Sloper and Dodge recoiled in horror. The upper part of the man had a waxy face, dull, fishy eyes, and dark hair; he lounged on the sofa like a corpse at ease, while his legs and feet stood by, leaning stiffly against the wall. The partners looked at him for a while in silence, and felt like two men haunted by a cast-iron ghost.

"Fix him together, for God's sake," said Dodge. "Don't leave him like that — he looks awful."

The genius grinned, and soon fixed the legs on.

"Now he looks better," said Dodge, poking about the figure. "Looks as much like life as most — ah, would you, you brute!" he exclaimed, springing back in alarm, for the figure had made a violent La Blanche swing at him.

"That's all right," said the genius, "that's a notion of my own. It's no good having his face knocked about, you know — lot of trouble to make that face. His head and body are all full of concealed springs, and if anybody hits him in the countenance, or in the pit of the stomach — favourite place to hit canvassers, the pit of the stomach — it sets a strong spring in motion, and he fetches his right hand round with a swipe that'll knock them into the middle of next week. It's an awful hit. Griffo couldn't dodge it, and Slavin couldn't stand against it. No fear of any man hitting *him* twice. And he's dog-proof too. His legs are padded with tar and oakum, and if a dog bites a bit out of him, it will take that dog the rest of his life to pick his teeth clean. Never bite anybody again, that dog won't. And he'll talk, talk, talk, like a pious conference gone mad; his phonograph can be charged for 100,000 times, and all you've got to do is to speak into it what you want him to say, and he'll say it. He'll go on saying it till he talks his man silly, or gets an order. He has an order form in his hand, and as soon as anyone signs it and gives it back to him, that sets another spring in motion, and he puts the order in his pocket, turns round, and walks away. Grand idea isn't he? Lor' bless you, I fairly love him.''

Evidently he did, for as he spoke the genius grinned affectionately at his monster.

''What about stairs?'' said Dodge.

''No stairs in the bush,'' said the inventor blowing a speck of dust off his apparition; ''all ground floor houses. Anyhow, if there were stairs we could carry him up and let him fall down afterwards, or get flung down like any other canvasser.''

''Ha! Let's see him walk,'' said Dodge.

The figure walked all right, stiff and erect.

''Now let's hear him yabber,'' was the next order.

Immediately the genius touched a spring, and a queer, tin-whistly voice issued from the creature's lips, and he began to sing, ''Little Annie Rooney.''

''Good!'' said Dodge, ''he'll do. We'll give you your price. Leave him here tonight, and come in tomorrow, and we'll start you off to some place in the back country with him. Have a cigar.''

And Mr Dodge, much elated, sucked at his pipe, and blew out through his nose a cloud of nearly solid smoke, which hung and floated about the door, and into which the genius walked as he sidled off. It fairly staggered him, and they could hear him sneezing and choking all the way downstairs. Then they locked up the office, and made for home, leaving the figure in readiness for his travels on the ensuing day.

Ninemile was a quiet little place, sleepy beyond description. When the mosquitoes in that town settled on anyone, they usually went to sleep, and forgot to bite him. The climate was so hot that the very grass-hoppers used to crawl into the hotel parlours out of the sun. There they would climb up the window curtains and go to sleep, and if anybody disturbed them they would fly into his eye with a great whizz, and drive the eye clean out at the back of his head. There was no likelihood of a public riot at Ninemile. The only thing that could rouse the inhabitants out of their lethargy was the prospect of a drink at somebody else's expense. And for those reasons it was decided to start the canvasser in this forgotten region; and then move him on to more populous and active localities if he proved a success. They sent up the genius, and a companion who knew the district well. The genius was to manage the automaton, and the other was to lay out the campaign, choose the victims, and collect the money, if they got any, geniuses being notoriously unreliable and loose in their cash. They got through a good deal of whisky on the way up, and when they arrived at Ninemile, they were in a cheerful mood, and disposed to take risks.

"Who'll we begin on?" said the genius.

"Oh, d—— it," said the other, "let's start on Macpherson."

Macpherson was the big bug of the place. He was a gigantic Scotchman, six feet four in his socks, freckled all over with freckles as big as half-crowns. His eyebrows would have made decent-sized moustaches even for a cavalryman, and his moustaches looked like horns. He was a fighter, from the ground up, and, moreover, he had a desperate "down" on canvassers generally and on Sloper and Dodge's canvassers in particular. This eminent firm had once published a book called *Remarkable Colonials*, and Macpherson had written out his own biography for it. He was intensely proud of his pedigree, and his grand relations, and in his narrative made out that he was descended from the original Pherson or Fhairshon who swam round Noah's Ark with his title deeds in his teeth. He showed how his people had fought under Alexander the Great and Timour, and had come over to England some centuries before the Conqueror. He also proved that he was related in a general way to one emperor, fifteen kings, twenty-five dukes, and earls and lords and viscounts innumerable. He dilated on the splendour of the family estates in Scotland, and the vast wealth of his relatives and progenitors. And then, after all, Sloper and Dodge managed to mix him up with some other fellow, some low-bred Irish ruffian who drove a corporation cart! Macpherson's biography gave it forth to the astonished town that he was born in Dublin of poor but honest parents, that his father when a youth had lived by selling matches, until one day he chanced to pick up a cigar end, and, emboldened by the possession of so much capital, had got married, and the product was Macpherson.

It was a terrible outrage. Macpherson at once became president for the whole of the western districts of the *Remarkable Colonials* Defence League, the same being a fierce and homicidal association got up to resist, legally and otherwise, paying for the books. Also, he had sworn by all he held sacred that every canvasser who came to harry him in future should die, and he had put up a notice on his office door, "Canvassers come in here at their own risk". He had a dog which he called a dog of the "hold 'em" breed, and this dog could tell a canvasser by his walk, and would go for him on sight. The reader will understand, therefore, that when the genius and his mate proposed to start on Macpherson, they were laying out a capacious contract for the cast-iron canvasser, and were taking a step which could only have been inspired by a morbid craving for excitement, aided by the influence of backblock whisky.

The genius wound the figure up in the back parlour of the pub. There were a frightful lot of screws to tighten before the thing would work, but at last he said it was ready, and they shambled off down the street, the figure marching stiffly between them. It had a book stuck under its arm and an order form in its hand. When they arrived opposite Macpherson's office (he was a land agent and had a ground-floor room) the genius started the phonograph working, pointed the figure straight at Macpherson's door and set it going, and then the two conspirators waited like Guy Fawkes in his cellar.

The figure marched across the road and in at the open door, talking to itself loudly in a hoarse, unnatural voice.

Macpherson was writing at his table and looked up.

The figure walked bang through a small collection of flower-pots, sent a chair flying, tramped heavily in the spittoon, and then brought up against the table with a loud crash and stood still. It was talking all the time.

"I have here," it said, "a most valuable work, a map and geography of Australia, which I desire to submit to your notice. The large and increasing demand of bush residents for time payment works has induced the publishers of this —"

"My God!" said Macpherson, "it's a canvasser. Here, Tom Sayers, Tom Sayers!" and he whistled and called for the dog. "Now," he said, "will you go out of this office quietly, or will you be thrown out? It's for yourself to decide, but you've only got while a duck wags his tail to decide in. Which'll it be?"

— "works of modern ages," said the canvasser. "Every person subscribing to this invaluable work will receive, in addition, a flat-iron, a railway pass for a year, and a pocket compass. If you will please sign this order —"

Just here Tom Sayers, the bulldog, came tearing through the office, and, without waiting for orders, hitched straight onto the calf of the canvasser's leg. To Macpherson's intense amazement the piece came clear away, and Tom Sayers rolled about the floor with his mouth full of some sticky substance which seemed to surprise him badly.

The long Scotchman paused awhile before this mystery, but at last he fancied he had got the solution. "Got a cork leg, have you?" said he. — "Well, let's see if your ribs are cork, too," and he struck the canvasser a terrific blow on the fifth button of the waistcoat.

Quicker than the lightning's flash came that terrific right-handed cross-counter. It was so quick that Macpherson never even knew what happened to him. He remembered striking his blow, and afterwards all was a blank. As a matter of fact, the canvasser's right hand, which had been adjusted by the genius for a high blow, landed just on the butt of Macpherson's ear and dropped him like a fowl. The gasping and terrified bulldog fled from the scene, and the canvasser stood over his fallen foe and droned on about the virtues of his publication, stating that he had come there merely as a friend, and to give the inhabitants of Ninemile a chance to buy a book which had already earned the approval of Dan O'Connor and the Earl of Jersey.

The genius and his mate watched this extraordinary drama through the window. They had kept up their courage with whisky and other stimulants, and now looked upon the whole affair as a wildly hilarious joke.

"By Gad! he's done him," said the genius as Macpherson went down, "done him in one hit. If he don't pay as a canvasser I'll take him to town and back him to fight Joe Goddard. Look out for yourself; don't you handle him!" he continued as the other approached the figure. "Leave him to me. As like as not, if you get fooling about him, he'll give you a smack in the snout that'll paralyse you."

So saying, he guided the automaton out of the office and into the street, and walked straight into — a policeman.

By a common impulse the genius and his mate at once ran rapidly away in different directions, and left the figure alone with the officer.

He was a fully ordained sergeant, by name Aloysius O'Grady; a squat, rosy little Irishman. He hated violent arrests and all that sort of thing, and had a faculty of persuading drunks and disorderlies and other fractious persons to "go quietly along with him", that was little short of marvellous. Excitable revellers, who were being carried along by their mates, struggling violently, would break away from their companions, and prance gaily along to the lock-up with the sergeant, whom, as likely as not, they would try to kiss on the way. Obstinate drunks who would do nothing but lie on the ground and kick their feet in the air, would get up like birds, serpent-charmed, and go with him to durance vile. As soon as he saw the canvasser, and noted his fixed, unearthly stare, and listened to his hoarse, unnatural voice, he knew what was the matter — it was a man in the horrors, a common enough spectacle at Ninemile. The sergeant resolved to decoy him into the lock-up, and accosted him in a friendly and free-and-easy way.

"Good day t'ye," he said.

"— Most magnificent volume ever published, jewelled in fourteen holes, working on a ruby roller, and in a glass case," said the book canvasser. "The likenesses of the historical personages are so natural that the book must not be left open on the table, or the mosquitoes will ruin it by stinging the faces of the portraits."

It then dawned on the sergeant that he was dealing with a book canvasser.

"Ah, sure," he said, "what's the use of tryin' to sell books at all, at all, folks does be peltin' them out into the street, and the nanny-goats lives on them these times. I sent the childher out to pick 'em up, and we have 'em at my place now — barrowloads of 'em. Come along wid me now, and I'll make you nice and comfortable for the night," and he laid his hand on the outstretched palm of the figure.

It was a fatal mistake. By so doing he set in motion the machinery which operated the figure's left arm, and it moved that limb in towards its body, and hugged the sergeant to its breast, with a vice-like grip. Then it started in a faltering, and uneven, but dogged way to walk towards the steep bank of the river, carrying the sergeant along with it.

"Immortal Saints!" gasped the sergeant, "he's squazin' the livin' breath out of me. Lave go now loike a dacent sowl, lave go. And oh, for the love of God, don't be shpakin' into my ear that way"; for the figure's mouth was pressed tight against the sergeant's ear, and its awful voice went through and through the little man's head, as it held forth about the volume. The sergeant struggled violently, and by so doing set some more springs in motion, and the figure's right arm made terrific swipes in the air. A following of boys and loafers had collected by this time. "Bly me, how he does lash out!" was the admiring remark they made. But they didn't altogether like interfering, notwithstanding the sergeant's frantic appeals, and things would have gone hard with him had his subordinate Constable Dooley not appeared on the scene.

Dooley, better known to the town boys as the "Wombat", from his sleepy disposition, was a man of great strength. He had originally been quartered at Redfern, Sydney, and had fought many bitter battles with the Bondi Push, the Black Red Push, and the Surry Hills Push. After this the duty at Ninemile was child's play, and he never ran in less than two drunks at a time; it was beneath his dignity to be seen capturing a solitary inebriate. If they wouldn't come any other way, he would take them by the ankles and drag them after him. The townsfolk would have cheerfully backed him to arrest John L. Sullivan if necessary; and when he saw the sergeant in the grasp of an inebriate he bore down on the fray full of fight.

"I'll soon make him lave ye go, sergeant," he said, and he tried to catch hold of the figure's right arm, to put on the "police twist". Unfortunately at that exact moment the sergeant's struggles touched one of the springs in the creature's breast with more than usual force. With the suddenness and severity of a horse kick, it lashed out with its right hand, catching the redoubtable Dooley a regular thud on the jaw, and sending him to grass, as if he had been shot. For a few minutes he "lay as only dead men lie". Then he got up bit by bit, and wandered off home to the police barracks, and mentioned casually to his wife that John L. Sullivan had come to town, and had taken the sergeant away to drown him. After which, having given orders that if anybody called that visitor was to be told he had gone out of town fifteen miles to serve a summons on a man for not registering a dog, he locked himself into a cell for the rest of the day.

Meanwhile, the canvasser, still holding the sergeant tightly clutched to its breast, was marching straight towards the river. Something had disorganised the voice arrangements, and it was now positively shrieking at the sergeant's ear, and, as it yelled, the little man yelled louder, "I don't want yer accursed book. Lave go of me, I say!" He beat with his fists on its face, and kicked at its shins without the slightest avail. A short, staggering rush, a wild shriek from the officer, and the two of them toppled over the steep bank and went souse into the bottomless depths of the Ninemile Creek.

That was the end of the whole matter. The genius and his mate returned to town hurriedly, and lay low, expecting to be indicted for murder. Constable Dooley drew up a report for the Chief of Police, which contained so many strange and unlikely statements that the department concluded the sergeant must have got drunk and drowned himself, and that Dooley saw him do it, but was too drunk to pull him out. Anyone unacquainted with Ninemile would have expected that a report of the occurrence would have reached the Sydney papers. As a matter of fact the storekeeper did think about writing a report, but decided that it was too much trouble. There was some idea of asking the Government to fish the two bodies out of the river, but about that time an agitation was started in Ninemile to have the Federal capital located there, and the other thing was forgotten. The genius drank himself to death; the "Wombat" became Sub-Inspector of Police; and a vague tradition about "a bloke who came up here in the horrors, and drownded poor old O'Grady'', is the only memory that remains of that wonderful creation, the cast-iron canvasser.

As for the canvasser himself there is a rusted mass far down in the waters of the creek, and in its arms it holds a skeleton dressed in the rags of what was once a police uniform. And on calm nights the passers-by sometimes imagine they can hear, rising out of the green and solemn depths, a husky, slushy voice, like that of an iron man with mud and weeds and dishcloths in his throat, and that voice is still urging the skeleton to buy a book in monthly parts. But the canvasser's utterance is becoming weak and used up in these days, and it is only when the waters are low and the air is profoundly still that he can be heard at all.

The Man from Snowy River

There was movement at the station, for the word had passed around
  That the colt from old Regret had got away,
And had joined the wild bush horses — he was worth a thousand pound,
So all the cracks had gathered to the fray.
All the tried and noted riders from the stations near and far
Had mustered at the homestead overnight,
For the bushmen love hard riding where the wild bush horses are,
And the stockhorse snuffs the battle with delight.

There was Harrison, who made his pile when Pardon won the cup,
The old man with his hair as white as snow;
But few could ride beside him when his blood was fairly up —
He would go wherever horse and man could go.
And Clancy of the Overflow came down to lend a hand,
No better horseman ever held the reins;
For never horse could throw him while the saddle girths would stand,
He learnt to ride while droving on the plains.

And one was there, a stripling on a small and weedy beast,
He was something like a racehorse undersized,
With a touch of Timor pony — three parts thoroughbred at least —
And such as are by mountain horsemen prized.
He was hard and tough and wiry — just the sort that won't say die —
There was courage in his quick impatient tread;
And he bore the badge of gameness in his bright and fiery eye,
And the proud and lofty carriage of his head.

But still so slight and weedy, one would doubt his power to stay,
And the old man said, ''That horse will never do
For a long and tiring gallop — lad, you'd better stop away,
Those hills are far too rough for such as you.''
So he waited sad and wistful — only Clancy stood his friend —
''I think we ought to let him come,'' he said;
''I warrant he'll be with us when he's wanted at the end,
For both his horse and he are mountain bred.

"He hails from Snowy River, up by Kosciusko's side,
Where the hills are twice as steep and twice as rough,
Where a horse's hoofs strike firelight from the flint stones every stride,
The man that holds his own is good enough.
And the Snowy River riders on the mountains make their home,
Where the river runs those giant hills between;
I have seen full many horsemen since I first commenced to roam,
But nowhere yet such horsemen have I seen."

So he went — they found the horses by the big mimosa clump —
They raced away towards the mountain's brow,
And the old man gave his orders, "Boys, go at them from the jump,
No use to try for fancy riding now.
And, Clancy, you must wheel them, try and wheel them to the right.
Ride boldly, lad, and never fear the spills,
For never yet was rider that could keep the mob in sight,
If once they gain the shelter of those hills."

So Clancy rode to wheel them — he was racing on the wing
Where the best and boldest riders take their place,
And he raced his stockhorse past them, and he made the ranges ring
With the stockwhip, as he met them face to face.
Then they halted for a moment, while he swung the dreaded lash,
But they saw their well-loved mountain full in view,
And they charged beneath the stockwhip with a sharp and sudden dash,
And off into the mountain scrub they flew.

Then fast the horsemen followed, where the gorges deep and black
Resounded to the thunder of their tread,
And the stockwhips woke the echoes, and they fiercely answered back
From cliffs and crags that beetled overhead.
And upward, ever upward, the wild horses held their way,
Where mountain ash and kurrajong grew wide;
And the old man muttered fiercely, "We may bid the mob good day,
No man can hold them down the other side."

When they reached the mountain's summit, even Clancy took a pull,
It well might make the boldest hold their breath,
The wild hop scrub grew thickly, and the hidden ground was full
Of wombat holes, and any slip was death.
But the man from Snowy River let the pony have his head,
And he swung his stockwhip round and gave a cheer,
And he raced him down the mountain like a torrent down its bed,
While the others stood and watched in very fear.

He sent the flint stones flying, but the pony kept his feet,
He cleared the fallen timber in his stride,
And the man from Snowy River never shifted in his seat —
It was grand to see that mountain horseman ride.
Through the stringybarks and saplings, on the rough and broken ground,
Down the hillside at a racing pace he went;
And he never drew the bridle till he landed safe and sound,
At the bottom of that terrible descent.

He was right among the horses as they climbed the further hill,
And the watchers on the mountain standing mute,
Saw him ply the stockwhip fiercely, he was right among them still,
As he raced across the clearing in pursuit.
Then they lost him for a moment, where two mountain gullies met
In the ranges, but a final glimpse reveals
On a dim and distant hillside the wild horses racing yet,
With the man from Snowy River at their heels.

And he ran them single-handed till their sides were white with foam.
He followed like a bloodhound on their track,
Till they halted cowed and beaten, then he turned their heads for home,
And alone and unassisted brought them back.
But his hardy mountain pony he could scarcely raise a trot,
He was blood from hip to shoulder from the spur;
But his pluck was still undaunted, and his courage fiery hot,
For never yet was mountain horse a cur.

And down by Kosciusko, where the pine-clad ridges raise
Their torn and rugged battlements on high,
Where the air is clear as crystal, and the white stars fairly blaze
At midnight in the cold and frosty sky,
And where around The Overflow the reed beds sweep and sway
To the breezes, and the rolling plains are wide,
The man from Snowy River is a household word today,
And the stockmen tell the story of his ride.

The Man from Snowy River

But the man from Snowy River let the pony have his head,
And he swung his stockwhip round and gave a cheer   *page 15*

Allalong Children

. . . but once he found his feet he took charge of the place, chased the lambs and the dogs, and wound up by chasing the cook out of the kitchen.

Illalong Children

ARRIVAL at "ILLALONG"

WHEN I was seven years old, my Uncle John died and my father took charge at "Illalong", the family's mountain station near Yass. Most parts of Australia are flat and dry, but this was hilly and wet. Some of the hills were very steep and rough with big patches of scrub where the kangaroos lay about in the shade during the heat of the day, just like shearers having a smoke during a spell. They threw themselves down on the ground in unstudied attitudes or they squatted on their haunches just as a shearer will sit on his heels, and some muscular shearers only need tails to be very like kangaroos, or, if a kangaroo had no tail, he would make a very passable shearer.

The young kangaroos, leaving their mothers' pouches, ran little races against each other over the rocks, round the big dead tree and back again, causing their mothers some worry lest they should bruise the pads of their hind feet on the rocks or jump across the wombat holes instead of going round them.

A wombat hole looks as though some unskilful person had sunk a shaft for gold, and is generally masked by long grass so that it is just the sort of place which might give anyone a very nasty fall. Not that this would worry the wombat, for he has his suite of rooms right away down at the bottom of his burrow and he never worries about anything. He avoids all thought so carefully that if he wants to move out of his bedroom into his sitting-room, he just stops where he is: it saves trouble.

In some parts of these hills, too, there were sheer cliff walls where a fall meant a very bad smash indeed, but the little kangaroos kept away from these dangerous places. These cliffs were the home of the rock wallabies, queerly marked little fellows scarcely bigger than squirrels, with long, furry tails and with patches of colour over their eyes. They had no fear of the cliffs; in fact, they loved nothing so well as to start at the foot of a cliff and go up it, just touching a knob of rock here or getting a foothold in a tiny crack there, till they came to the top. The other animals were envious of these displays and thought that the rock wallabies were very flash people. Flasher still were the lyrebirds which spread their tails and pranced up and down on an open patch of rock, mimicking and making fun of every creature in the bush. If the lyrebirds heard a new sound such as the crash of a splitter's axe or the tinkle of a bullock bell, they would practise it until they got it right; but they did not need to practise such sounds as the alarm cry of young parrots in a nest, causing the parrot mothers to hurry home to see what had gone wrong. What with one thing and another, the lyrebirds gave their neighbours a lot of trouble.

The "Illalong" homestead was an old-fashioned cottage, built of slabs covered with plaster, whitewashed till it shone in the sun. The roof had originally been bark and when the bark got old and friable the bullock driver and Kerry the black boy would be sent out with axes to strip some more. They stripped it by cutting a seam down the side of a tree and then they wedged and hammered the bark until it became loose and at last it peeled off in a cylinder. They flattened this out and put logs on it so that it could not curl up again, and after a few days, when it had dried nice and flat, they went out with the bullock dray and brought in the load. Then they pulled the old bark off and stuck the new bark in place and, lo, they had a new roof. Then came the day when the dray arrived with a load of galvanised iron to make a permanent roof and this was put on over the bark for the sake of coolness. When it was first erected, the wild ducks, flying through the moonlight, would sometimes mistake the shining roof for a sheet of water and would land on it, thump, thump, thump, waking everybody out of their sleep and terrifying the ducks, who were quite ashamed of themselves for having made such a mistake. They soon learned the difference between a sheet of iron and a sheet of water and the roof gave every satisfaction, except that the possums would scamper backwards and forwards along the ridgepole and sometimes one of them would miss his footing and would slide down to the water-spouting, with his claws making the most frightful scratching sound. When one of them did this, the others would all chatter at him in their queer lingo, making fun of him, and the possum who had slid down would sit on the spouting at the edge of the verandah with his tail hanging over and would explain that this sort of roof was no good, a man couldn't get his claws into it. If anybody pulled his tail he would start straight up the roof again and would slip back, making more noise than ever.

The homestead ceilings were made of calico, whereon the possums used to run races in the evenings before going out into the garden for a feed. The children took a hand by trying to stick sharp instruments into the feet of the possums as they raced across the ceiling. On leaving the house, the possums used to jump from the roof onto a paling fence and run along it till they could leap into the foliage of a big elderberry tree. Armed with sticks, we youngsters used to wait under the shelter of the verandah and try to knock the possums off as they ran past. Brother Possum, however, has a keen eye at night and would only make his rush when his enemies had their minds distracted. They were quaint little fellows, the possums, with their inquisitive faces and their friendly ways. Gum leaves were their natural food, which gave them a fine aromatic eucalyptus smell; but they preferred fruit when they could get it, and small blame to them, for gum leaves must become very monotonous.

Among the night noises were the call of a mopoke, the whine of a native cat, or the bloodcurdling hooting of a powerful owl. The first time that one of these birds really let his voice go in the garden my father happened to be away, and nobody in the place could guess the source of these dreadful sounds. The girl in the kitchen, bush-reared, came in and explained matters. "Don't you know what that is?" she said. "It's a howl." We were just going to ask her what was howling, when a great grey bird on noiseless wings drifted across the yard just over our heads and the banshee myth that might have been was exploded. At that, a powerful owl can give any banshee that ever lived a start and beat it at its own speciality.

Jack and I were just learning to ride on quiet station ponies, and we had, like our Scottish forebears, to contend with raiders. Not armed raiders, be it understood, but every year in the spring there flowed past the station a tide of shearers making out to the western sheds. Mostly they were mounted, but some were on foot, and these footsloggers had a habit of helping themselves to any quiet horse which they could catch in the paddock at night. These they would turn loose when they reached their destination and it was a matter of luck and police efficiency if they were ever recovered.

Horses were cheap enough, two pounds was about the average price for a good station pony; but it would have been a heartbreaking business if our mounts had disappeared. We took counsel from "Old Harry", not the mythical personage of that name, but as stout a retainer as ever served a Scotsman. Old Harry was an English agricultural labourer who had been "sent out" for poaching pheasants, and was a match for any raider. He was a "Zummerzet" man. "Pit yeer pownies in garden every night," he said, "and t'dorgs'll let ye know if owt comes after 'em." Not only did we retain our ponies, but at the ages of about six and seven respectively we bought a horse for ourselves.

A man who described himself as "an overlander who had just delivered some cattle" came into the station one day, leading a horse so poor and weak that it could hardly stagger along. The overlander, whose motto appeared to be "Keep going", said that he would sell the horse if anyone would give him five shillings to cover his fare to Yass in the coach.

Everyone in authority was away, but there had been rain at the station and the old sheep yard at the back of the stables was covered with shoots of beautiful soft young herbage. We somehow raked up five shillings between us, and with the assistance of Old Harry, who knew nothing about horses, actually propped the animal up with a pole and fed it with handfuls of herbage. After it had eaten a good feed, we very reluctantly let it lie down.

Some hour or two later, we decided to get it up again, but Old Harry had gone away and we were unable to lift it. Then it suddenly struck us that the horse could eat just as well while lying on the ground; in fact, it seemed to prefer it, and for the rest of that day and the next we were carrying food to the patient. When my father came home, the horse could get up by himself, and could even walk about in a staggering sort of way.

"I don't mind your buying him," said father, "but I think your overlander must have found a horse which nobody had lost. I know his brand. He is a Queensland horse and I suppose the overlander was about a hundred miles ahead of the police. That horse might have belonged to some little boy like yourselves, and you wouldn't like a little Queensland boy to keep your ponies if anyone took them away. I'll have to write to the owner." Two very gloomy boys waited till an answer came to that letter.

"The boys can keep the horse," it said, "but we would like to get hold of the man who pinched him. We have hundreds of horses up here, too many. If the boys are in the horse buying business, we can let them have as many as they want at five bob a head. We used to call that horse White-when-he's-wanted because the black boy who broke him in said, 'By cripes, boss, this fella white when he's wanted.' Tell the boys to go down to his fetlocks as if they were going to take hobbles off him when they want to catch him. All our horses are broken in that way, and when he freshens up he might give them a lot of trouble if they tried to catch him any other way. Good luck."

When he recovered his health and strength, the Queenslander soon showed that he was no small boy's horse. He threw a visiting jackaroo and tried to strike him with his front feet while on the ground, a manoeuvre which the jackaroo foiled by rolling under a log. Then the horse was tried in harness, on the theory that he must have been created for some useful purpose. To everyone's amazement he went away as quietly as possible, nor did he ever misbehave himself except on the occasion when the blacksmith's boy in Yass unfortunately selected him, in place of his yoke-mate, for a ride up the street. He went out for a short ride and he got it. "If I had known he was broke in by a black boy," he said, "I'd have blackened myself before I got on him."

That episode was closed by the sale of the horse (guaranteed quiet to harness only) for five pounds, a very nice profit on five shillings.

STOREKEEPING

*P*LAYING AT storekeeping has always a charm for children. One gets behind a counter which isn't there and sells tins of imaginary jam, fictitious frocks, and stones for bread to the indulgent buyer. The buyer proceeds to bestow the non-existent goods in a phantom shopping bag and makes a dignified exit.

Playing at shopkeeping is all very well in its way, but how much better was it, as we "Illalong" children did, to keep a real store and sell meat, flour, tea, sugar and tobacco to real live buyers?

What an aroma hung round the old slab and bark building — an aroma built up of the smell of new boots, harness and saddles of colonial manufacture. There was something all-pervading about the scent of colonial leather in the early days. Then there was the scent of black plug tobacco, so full of nicotine that the plugs stuck together in the hogshead and had to be pried apart with a chisel. The scent of sugar came about third in the list of odours, sugar so slightly removed from molasses that it was full of black sticky lumps, dearly beloved by the blacks. A few blankets, a few rolls of cotton cloth, pickles, jams, tea, sauces, bottles of Farmer's Friend and Painkiller and bags of flour made up the stock in trade — all utilities and no luxuries.

As the heads of the family had but little time to spare, most of the storekeeping was done by the two little girls, Flo and Jessie, then about eight and six years of age; somewhat early to begin storekeeping, one would say, but when a neighbour's boy of fourteen was running a mail contract for the Government, a girl of eight was considered quite competent to sell goods in a store.

Some of the customers were "travellers", i.e. men seeking work, and they were easily attended to, for the only thing they wanted to buy was tobacco. Meat, flour, sugar, tea, all these things were given free of charge in proportion to the needs of the traveller. In return, the travellers were expected to cut a certain amount of firewood, a request that would not have been made of them at the big "outside" Queensland stations, but "Illalong" was an "inside station", and a little work was expected of every traveller in return for his dole.

Even the smaller of the two little girls could be given the key of the store and could be trusted to sell to a traveller. No choice was needed, for there was only one brand of tobacco. Quaint characters they were, these travellers, some with Oxford accents and some foreigners barely able to talk English; and the little girls were given jurisdiction to throw in a pair of old boots with a fig of tobacco when they saw the buyer's toes peeping out of his boots. Should a foot be badly chafed, the buyer would be told to go and camp by the creek for a day or two till he was fit to travel, and liberal dabs of ointment would be spread by infant fingers on pieces of linen rag to help the recovery. One might say, as was said of Beatrix Potter's Dormouse, that this was hardly the way to conduct a retail business, but it was the way that the children were encouraged to take, and none of them regretted in after life the lessons they had learnt in dealing with men at the store.

A brief "thank you" was about all that they ever heard from the travellers, but the station hands were more conversational. For instance, there was John Wilberforce Morley, one of the shepherds, reputed to be an Oxford man who had come down in the world. He never spoke of England, for they had their pride, these children of misfortune, but he must have had some friends in England in good circumstances. Someone sent him, all the way from England, a present of a Russian dog, and if there were many like this dog in Russia, one would feel sorry for the wolves in that country. Shaggy-coated, big-footed, nearly the size of a pony, he had an enormous head with powerful jaws, and he glared out upon the world through a fringe of hair which almost blinded him, but John Wilberforce Morley had an aptitude for dogs. One wonders whether Morley might have disguised his circumstances from his relatives and that they thought they were sending him a most useful present.

Possibly the dog had a certain value in Russia, for, in spite of his Bolshevik appearance, he had an aristocratic name and was registered in the Russian stud books as "Peter the Great". Morley was not a conversational character. It was his custom to walk into the store, buy what he wanted and go away again to the dreadful loneliness of his hut on the run without exchanging more than a word or two with the little girls, but the arrival of Peter the Great changed all that. On his first visit to the station after the dog's arrival he began to tell in instalments the saga of Peter the Great. This was the first instalment.

"I'm having a lot of trouble with that dog," he said. "He wanted to kill my old sheepdog right straight away. I had to take him out with the sheep on a lead till he got used to my old dog. And then the trouble of feeding him! He eats as much as a horse. Luckily the station sent me out a gun to shoot crows, so I knock over kangaroos and wallabies and crows and eaglehawks — anything. He even ate a porcupine after I'd skinned it. Well, it's time I was getting off home. Do you mind telling me what day of the week it is? I've forgotten."

His next instalment was encouraging. "Peter the Great is settling down," he said. "He hasn't chased anything for a long time, except a kangaroo dog which followed a hawker who came to the hut, and he had no chance in life of catching the kangaroo dog. I'll take half a dozen boxes of matches, please. He brushed all my matches into a bucket of water with his tail."

Then came the great adventure which set the seal on the fame of Peter the Great. This was before the days of paddocking, and the sheep were shut up in a yard each night. One morning very early, Morley was aroused by a great commotion at the sheep yard, so he loosed Peter the Great and ran out to find that a big cattle dog from a neighbouring station was in the yard, killing a sheep. Morley's old sheepdog was raising the alarm at the top of his voice, but could do nothing more. This cattle dog fancied himself the equal of any dog that ever stepped, but he had yet to meet a Russian. When he saw Peter the Great, he took to flight and would have got out through a gap in the yard, only that Morley's old sheepdog threw himself on him. Badly bitten, he hung onto the cattle dog long enough to let the slow-moving Peter the Great sink his teeth into the murderer's windpipe, and that was the end of the cattle dog.

Morley had to tell this story to the children every time that he came up to the station, and he told it like an actor, playing the part of each dog in turn, bringing out the alarmed screams of the old sheepdog, the brutal worrying of the cattle dog and the grand finale of the entrance of Peter the Great. Perhaps he had been an actor, for no one ever heard Morley talk of his past: nor did he ever talk of his future until one day he came in and said, very briefly, that he would be leaving the shepherding, as he had been called back to England. He gave no further information, but he said that he would be taking the Russian dog to England with him and would be obliged if the children would look after his old sheepdog for the rest of its life.

From these facts one is able to deduce that Morley was moving into a very much higher sphere than that of a shepherd, and he would have at least one good tale to tell the children in England.

HOME LIFE

$\mathcal{B}$EFORE GOING any further on this journey, let us consider home life after the railway came; when we were at any rate partially civilised and got mail every day instead of once a week. Speaking of life in the bush, the Australian poet, Brunton Stephens, has told us that "this eucalyptic cloisterdom is anything but gay", but we managed to enjoy ourselves in our own way.

We outgrew the original homestead of four big rooms and some skillion rooms were added, but, as the family continued to grow, more space was needed, and a four-roomed house was brought in from the holding of a selector who had sold out to the station. This house, not a very large one, was jacked up onto rollers by the bullock driver and a bush carpenter, who were in charge of operations. We watched it coming through the trees swaying like a ship at sea, but holding together. Arrived after its voyage, there was some very delicate work with bullocks, hauling it onto its new foundations. When it is required to move a whole house an inch and a half, a bullock team is hardly the handiest method in the world, but the driver somehow made those bullocks understand what was wanted and when he spoke to them, never raising his voice, they would just put their weight into the yokes an ounce at a time. We children gave all the credit to the two leading bullocks, Rodney and Spot, whom we considered to be as knowing as men and a lot stronger. Slowly, slowly, the building slid into position and the bullock driver's reputation was made.

Compared with the western place, "Illalong" was poor country, but a previous owner had planted a garden with all sorts of English plants and trees, cypress, holly, hawthorn, and a glorious avenue of acacias. The orchard, too, was a delight, with its figs, walnuts, mulberry trees, cherries, grapes, apples and peaches. In a good season we would fill a clothes basket with grapes or figs, and when the clothes basket was filled there seemed to be just as much fruit as ever.

Sometimes the girls were afraid to gather the figs and grapes because of the bees and hornets which came in thousands to sip the juice from the ripening fruit. The Australian hornet is a man-at-arms, with his red and black banded uniform and his sting like the dagger of a bravo. Not that he would go out of his way to attack anybody, but he was a short-tempered gentleman, and if a small hand gathering fruit happened to touch him he would consider himself insulted and would use his dagger without waiting for apologies. One of the station boys said, "If it comes to being bit by a snake or stung by a hornet, give me the snake."

Then there were the birds who insisted on their rights to the fruit: little silver-eyes nibbling away industriously with their tiny beaks; parrots biting slices out of the peaches with their pincer-like jaws; and the leatherheads whose heads and necks were bare of feathers so that they would not get their plumage in a mess while digging into the fruit. We did not exactly grudge the birds their share but it was disconcerting, while sitting in a fork swaying perilously, to see the silver-eyes and parrots gorging away at the ripest plums and peaches which always grew at the ends of the branches, just out of our reach. The leatherheads were grey birds, bare-necked as vultures and not, apparently, gifted with any brains: and yet they were the most expert nest builders of the lot, weaving long grasses and strips of stringybark into beautiful hanging nests which swung from the twigs right out on the end of the gum tree branches where nobody could climb. Not even the iguana, that terror to small birds, dared trust his weight on the frail twigs where the leatherheads hung their nests, and they built them so high from the ground that Mr Iguana was due for a very nasty fall if the branches gave way with him.

Other fruit lovers were the bower birds, who must have had the collector's instinct, for they built bowers of sticks and lined them with grasses and decorated them with pieces of glass, coloured rags and bright stones. One can imagine the pride with which one bower bird showed to another the neck of a glass bottle, in the days when the necks of glass bottles were none too numerous. However, they did not let their mania for collecting interfere with their appetites and, if they were a hundred yards away, down at the bottom of the garden, they could scent an apple being peeled in the house and would fly up and sit on the window sill, hoping to get a share of the core or the peelings. They were very friendly people, the bower birds, and were quite prepared to have a fruit lunch with anybody.

But life was not all birds and fruit and flowers. We had to work fairly hard. The girls gathered eggs from the fowls which ran wild all over the place, scores and scores of them, nesting in old barns, under the water tanks, or living the life of Riley as wild birds, never coming near the house and nesting among the masses of variegated thistles in the old sheep yard. Dodging through these thistles after nests, it was nothing unusual to see half a dozen fowls rise up like rocketing pheasants and fly for a hundred yards or so, to the accompaniment of a chorus of cackles from their mates hidden away in the thistle bed. There were no foxes, and, as for the native cats, well, the fowls bred faster than the native cats could eat them. A hundred eggs in a day was just a fair tally, and these eggs had to be put away in lime water as a reserve against the cold weather. Motherless lambs were brought to the house and installed as pets, and when anyone went up the yard he was always beset by lambs wagging their tails and getting in his road. A motherless foal was brought in, shy and frightened at first; but once he felt his feet he took charge of the place, chased the lambs and the dogs, and wound up by chasing the cook out of the kitchen. After this exploit he was judged old enough to go out into the paddocks; and one day a Hindoo hawker came in badly rattled and said that a colt foal had "sparred up at him like a prize-fighter", and what sort of horses did we keep, anyhow?

The strongest character about the place was the pet white cockatoo known as "Uncle". He had been brought in by a black boy who had picked him up when he fell out of the parental nest in the spout of a tree and, as he was only able to flutter a few yards, the boy had caught him and brought him along. "Plenty savvy, that feller," said the boy. "Plenty talk, him know a lot, all same old man." At first he was most uninteresting, for his only accomplishment was to sit on a perch swaying himself backwards and forwards, keeping up a never-ending complaint "ah-ah-ah-ah" until we wondered that he did not get a sore throat.

Uncle's life seemed to be just one long complaint until one day we heard our father calling mother from the bottom of the garden. As we knew father was out on the run, it was inexplicable. We ran into the garden thinking that perhaps he had had a fall from his horse and was making his way home; and there we found the cockatoo practising the first words he had learned. His first impersonation was such a success that he soon learned to call the dogs by their names and they, regarding him as a superior intellect, never dared to interfere with him.

Cockatoos spend a lot of their time in digging for yams, and he soon learned to dig up plants or seeds; when washing was put out on the line he would wait till everyone had gone and then he would walk along the clothes line like a man on a tightrope, pulling out the clothes pegs and letting the washing drop on the ground and one day, when he had no other mischief on hand, he was found on the roof patiently loosening, with his powerful beak, the screws which held the sheets of galvanised iron in place. Because he was so full of knowledge, we had called him Uncle Remus, and father said that he was a blessing in disguise for it kept everyone interested to know what he was doing and gave them something to talk about. At any hour of the day someone was liable to say, "What's Uncle doing?" and it generally turned out that he was in some mischief or other. Sometimes Uncle would go for a fly round the house, but if he went out into the paddocks, the wild cockatoos would have none of him and he had to make the best of his way home, shrieking for help. After these exploits he might be heard whispering softly to himself, like one whose brain has been turned by much meditation. Then he would burst into maniac shrieks of disgust which would be heard a mile away, had there been anyone to hear him.

THE RESCUE

FOR TWO years in succession, Mr and Mrs Tom-tit had built a nest in the pepper tree within ten feet of the homestead. It was safer there than out in the bush where native cats, crows, and sparrowhawks made the lives of small birds very precarious. And then a third year arrived and they returned to the old pepper tree, which had served them so well in the past.

To the human eye, there did not seem much wrong with either of the two old nests. True, the wind and weather had knocked them out of shape; the linings where the previous families had been reared were very worn and likely to let the wind through on the eggs; but the framework, if such a term could be applied to a structure of grass, was quite intact. Could it be repaired for this year's nest?

And it is just here where small birds differ from human beings. Humans resort to all sorts of devices to avoid trouble; little birds find pleasure in the work of building a nest, so a new nest it had to be and the pair started to twist their grass stems and invaluable bits of thread, so easy to handle, as mooring ropes round the twigs of the pepper tree.

The small architects must have felt annoyed when a dry stick fell from one of the upper branches of the tree right onto their nest, but this proved a windfall in every sense, for the ends of the stick were securely caught in the branches. They at once moored their nest to it, thus getting a foundation for the top of their nest, while a twig about an eighth of an inch in diameter gave support at the lower end. There was much twittering until this decision was arrived at, but once the point was settled the building went on with great speed. These particular tom-tits always build a nest with a lower and upper compartment. In the lower the hen hatches her eggs and rears her young, while the upper compartment is, in the opinion of the bush people, built with the idea of deceiving the cuckoos, who have a pernicious habit of laying an egg in other birds' nests. A cuckoo's egg laid in the upper compartment would do nobody any harm.

By and by came hatching time, and then the troubles of the tom-tits were trebled. From dawn till dark they toiled, bringing infinitely small mouthfuls of microscopical food to their family. Then came the day when the family, fully fledged duplicates of their parents, were ready to go on their first solo flight. They had strengthened their wings by short experimental flights from one twig to another.

Now came the great adventure.

Do parent birds talk, and do child birds listen? The parents made plenty of noise, chirping excitedly, but the babies appeared as dazed as young aeroplanists going up for the first time. At last one took his courage in hand and followed his mother to the nearest tree, crossing a small pond en route. It was a short enough flight, but when one is very small indeed a flight across a small pond takes on the appearance of crossing the Atlantic.

Two others made the trip safely, but there is always a backward child in every family, and the last of the brood put no style into his work. He fluttered desperately and might have got across only that a puff of wind checked him just when he was most tired and, like a piece of windblown thistle leaf, he fell right into the centre of the pond.

It was a frightful situation. The parents sounded their alarm notes (quite different from their ordinary twitter), but what chance was there of making themselves understood?

It so happened that there was a chance. Flo and Jessie were playing in the garden with old Nan, the Irish setter, an unappreciated artist if ever there was one. Father was too busy to look after her education and we children had no knowledge of a setter's gifts. Nan, quite untrained, would "set" to a quail in the garden and we would say, "Go on, Nan, what are you stopping for?"

After a time Nan gave us up as hopeless and took to following anybody who left the station on a horse. One would expect a setter to be a restful sort of animal, but Nan was a sort of canine steam engine, ranging wide of the horse for hour after hour, covering incredible distances in a day. Every now and again she would scent game, a kangaroo rat sleeping in his little grass nest or a curlew standing immobile, hoping to be unnoticed. These Nan would set for a few seconds, always hoping for a word of command. Getting no orders, she would resume her headlong sorties.

Canine artists such as gun dogs and sheepdogs are born with the urge to work, to exhibit whatever talent Nature has given them. Failing anyone to take an interest in him, a young sheepdog will herd fowls from one enclosure to another, and a young gun dog will "set" or "point" whatever sort of game comes before him. Poor old Nan! She would lie before the fire in the winter evenings, whimpering in her dreams over her wasted gifts.

Young as the girls were, they had learned to distinguish the notes of birds, so they set off, followed by Nan, to see what was happening. They soon saw that a very small bird was drowning before their eyes, and the pool was forbidden water to the children, but children in the bush learn to think things out for themselves.

The problem was to get Nan to go in for the little bird, and suddenly Flo had a brainwave. She stooped down and picked up a stone and threw it into the pool alongside the struggling infant. Nan saw the splash and bounded in like a Newfoundland dog going to rescue a drowning boy.

When Nan reached the place where she had seen the splash, the stone had disappeared and nothing was left on the pool but the baby tom-tit, almost too small to be worth retrieving; but rather than make a fruitless voyage, she thought she might as well bring home the bird. Fortunately, her instinct had taught her to take the greatest care of everything that she retrieved — she would even carry an egg in her mouth without breaking it — and the little bird disappeared in one gulp of the great red slobbery mouth and she headed for the shore. The parents raised a more agonised squawk than ever when they saw their child gulped down by a marine monster, but they need not have worried. The bird was as safe in Nan's mouth as if it were in the nest. Three strokes of her great limbs and she walked up the bank of the pool and dropped a bedraggled but uninjured bird at the feet of the children. This stirred the parent birds to a last outburst of clamour; after seeing their offspring delivered from a marine monster, it was now to meet a dreadful death at the hands of a land monster.

Carefully, Flo dried it with her handkerchief and put it on a stump well away from the water. The old birds flew down and fussed over it till it was strong enough to flutter up to the nest, and the episode was ended. The only sad thing about the whole affair was that the old setter, Nan, never knew that she had saved a life.

On Kiley's Run

The roving breezes come and go
    On Kiley's Run,
The sleepy river murmurs low,
And far away one dimly sees
Beyond the stretch of forest trees —
Beyond the foothills dusk and dun —
The ranges sleeping in the sun
    On Kiley's Run.

'Tis many years since first I came
    To Kiley's Run,
More years than I would care to name
Since I, a stripling, used to ride
For miles and miles at Kiley's side,
The while in stirring tones he told
The stories of the days of old
    On Kiley's Run.

I see the old bush homestead now
    On Kiley's Run,
Just nestled down beneath the brow
Of one small ridge above the sweep
Of river flat, where willows weep
And jasmine flowers and roses bloom,
The air was laden with perfume
    On Kiley's Run.

We lived the good old station life
    On Kiley's Run,
With little thought of care or strife.
Old Kiley seldom used to roam,
He liked to make the Run his home,
The swagman never turned away
With empty hand at close of day
    From Kiley's Run.

We kept a racehorse now and then
   On Kiley's Run,
And neighb'ring stations brought their men
To meetings where the sport was free,
And dainty ladies came to see
Their champions ride; with laugh and song
The old house rang the whole night long
   On Kiley's Run.

The station hands were friends I wot
   On Kiley's Run,
A reckless, merry-hearted lot —
All splendid riders, and they knew
The ''boss'' was kindness through and through.
Old Kiley always stood their friend,
And so they served him to the end
   On Kiley's Run.

But droughts and losses came apace
   To Kiley's Run,
Till ruin stared him in the face;
He toiled and toiled while lived the light,
He dreamed of overdrafts at night:
At length, because he could not pay,
His bankers took the stock away
   From Kiley's Run.

Old Kiley stood and saw them go
   From Kiley's Run.
The well-bred cattle marching slow;
His stockmen, mates for many a day,
They wrung his hand and went away.
Too old to make another start,
Old Kiley died — of broken heart,
   On Kiley's Run.

The owner lives in England now
   Of Kiley's Run.
He knows a racehorse from a cow;
But that is all he knows of stock:
His chiefest care is how to dock
Expenses, and he sends from town
To cut the shearers' wages down
   On Kiley's Run.

There are no neighbours anywhere
   Near Kiley's Run.
The hospitable homes are bare,
The gardens gone; for no pretence
Must hinder cutting down expense:
The homestead that we held so dear
Contains a half-paid overseer
   On Kiley's Run.

All life and sport and hope have died
   On Kiley's Run.
No longer there the stockmen ride;
For sour-faced boundary riders creep
On mongrel horses after sheep,
Through ranges where, at racing speed,
Old Kiley used to "wheel the lead"
   On Kiley's Run.

There runs a lane for thirty miles
   Through Kiley's Run.
On either side the herbage smiles,
But wretched trav'lling sheep must pass
Without a drink or blade of grass
Thro' that long lane of death and shame:
The weary drovers curse the name
   Of Kiley's Run.

The name itself is changed of late
   Of Kiley's Run.
They call it "Chandos Park Estate".
The lonely swagman through the dark
Must hump his swag past Chandos Park.
The name is English, don't you see,
The old name sweeter sounds to me
   Of "Kiley's Run".

I cannot guess what fate will bring
   To Kiley's Run —
For chances come and changes ring —
I scarcely think 'twill always be
Locked up to suit an absentee;
And if he lets it out in farms
His tenants soon will carry arms
   On Kiley's Run.

On Riley's Run

The swagman never turned away
With empty hand at close of day   page 30

A Bush Christening

"Poke a stick up the log, give the spalpeen a prog . . ."   page 34

A Bush Christening

On the outer Barcoo where the churches are few,
    And men of religion are scanty,
On a road never cross'd 'cept by folk that are lost,
    One Michael Magee had a shanty.

Now this Mike was the dad of a ten-year-old lad,
    Plump, healthy, and stoutly conditioned;
He was strong as the best, but poor Mike had no rest
    For the youngster had never been christened.

And his wife used to cry, "If the darlin' should die
    Saint Peter would not recognise him."
But by luck he survived till a preacher arrived,
    Who agreed straightaway to baptise him.

Now the artful young rogue, while they held their collogue,
    With his ear to the keyhole was listenin',
And he muttered in fright while his features turned white,
    "What the divil and all is this christenin'?"

He was none of your dolts, he had seen them brand colts,
    And it seemed to his small understanding,
If the man in the frock made him one of the flock,
    It must mean something very like branding.

So away with a rush he set off for the bush,
    While the tears in his eyelids they glistened —
"'Tis outrageous," says he, "to brand youngsters like me,
    I'll be dashed if I'll stop to be christened!"

Like a young native dog he ran into a log,
    And his father with language uncivil,
Never heeding the "praste" cried aloud in his haste,
    "Come out and be christened, you divil!"

But he lay there as snug as a bug in a rug,
    And his parents in vain might reprove him,
Till his reverence spoke (he was fond of a joke)
    "I've a notion," says he, "that'll move him."

"Poke a stick up the log, give the spalpeen a prog;
  Poke him aisy — don't hurt him or maim him,
'Tis not long that he'll stand, I've the water at hand,
  As he rushes out this end I'll name him.

"Here he comes, and for shame! ye've forgotten the name —
  Is it Patsy or Michael or Dinnis?"
Here the youngster ran out, and the priest gave a shout —
  "Take your chance, anyhow, wid 'Maginnis'!"

As the howling young cub ran away to the scrub
  Where he knew that pursuit would be risky,
The priest, as he fled, flung a flask at his head
  That was labelled "Maginnis's Whisky!"

And Maginnis Magee has been made a J.P.,
  And the one thing he hates more than sin is
To be asked by the folk who have heard of the joke,
  How he came to be christened "Maginnis"!

Old Pardon, the Son of Reprieve

You never heard tell of the story?
    Well, now, I can hardly believe!
Never heard of the honour and glory
    Of Pardon, the son of Reprieve?
But maybe you're only a Johnnie
    And don't know a horse from a hoe?
Well, well, don't get angry, my sonny,
    But, really, a young 'un should know.

They bred him out back on the "Never",
    His mother was Mameluke breed.·
To the front — and then stay there — was ever
    The root of the Mameluke creed.
He seemed to inherit their wiry
    Strong frames — and their pluck to receive —
As hard as a flint and as fiery
    Was Pardon, the son of Reprieve.

We ran him at many a meeting
    At crossing and gully and town,
And nothing could give him a beating —
    At least when our money was down.
For weight wouldn't stop him, nor distance,
    Nor odds, though the others were fast,
He'd race with a dogged persistence,
    And wear them all down at the last.

At the Turon the Yattendon filly
    Led by lengths at the mile and a half,
And we all began to look silly,
    While *her* crowd were starting to laugh;
But the old horse came faster and faster,
    His pluck told its tale, and his strength,
He gained on her, caught her, and passed her,
    And won it, hands down, by a length.

And then we swooped down on Menindie
    To run for the President's Cup —
Oh! that's a sweet township — a shindy
    To them is board, lodging, and sup.
Eye-openers they are, and their system
    Is never to suffer defeat;
It's "win, tie, or wrangle" — to best 'em
    You must lose 'em, or else it's "dead heat".

We strolled down the township and found 'em
    At drinking and gaming and play;
If sorrows they had, why they drowned 'em,
    And betting was soon under way.
Their horses were good 'uns and fit 'uns,
    There was plenty of cash in the town;
They backed their own horses like Britons,
    And Lord! how *we* rattled it down!

With gladness we thought of the morrow,
    We counted our wagers with glee,
A simile homely to borrow —
    "There was plenty of milk in our tea".
You see we were green; and we never
    Had even a thought of foul play,
Though we well might have known that the clever
    Division would "put us away".

Experience "*docet*", they tell us,
    At least so I've frequently heard,
But, "dosing" or "stuffing", those fellows
    Were up to each move on the board;
They got to his stall — it is sinful
    To think what such villains would do —
And they gave him a regular skinful
    Of barley — green barley — to chew.

He munched it all night, and we found him
    Next morning as full as a hog —
The girths wouldn't nearly meet round him;
    He looked like an overfed frog.
We saw we were done like a dinner —
    The odds were a thousand to one
Against Pardon turning up winner,
    'Twas cruel to ask him to run.

We got to the course with our troubles,
    A crestfallen couple were we;
And we heard the ''books'' calling the doubles —
    A roar like the surf of the sea;
And over the tumult and louder
    Rang, ''Any price Pardon, I lay!''
Says Jimmy, ''The children of Judah
    Are out on the warpath to-day.''

Three miles in three heats: Ah, my sonny
    The horses in those days were stout,
They had to run well to win money;
    I don't see such horses about.
Your six-furlong vermin that scamper
    Half a mile with their featherweight up;
They wouldn't earn much of their damper
    In a race like the President's Cup.

The first heat was soon set a-going;
    The Dancer went off to the front;
The Don on his quarters was showing,
    With Pardon right out of the hunt.
He rolled and he weltered and wallowed —
    You'd kick your hat faster, I'll bet;
They finished all bunched, and he followed
    All lathered and dripping with sweat.

But troubles came thicker upon us,
  For while we were rubbing him dry
The stewards came over to warn us:
  "We hear you are running a bye!
If Pardon don't spiel like tarnation
  And win the next heat — if he can —
He'll earn a disqualification;
  Just think over *that*, now, my man!"

Our money all gone and our credit,
  Our horse couldn't gallop a yard;
And then people thought that *we* did it!
  It really was terribly hard.
We were objects of mirth and derision
  To folk in the lawn and the stand,
And the yells of the clever division
  Of "Any price, Pardon!" were grand.

We still had a chance for the money,
  Two heats still remained to be run;
If both fell to us — why, my sonny,
  The clever division were done.
And Pardon was better, we reckoned,
  His sickness was passing away,
So he went to the post for the second
  And principal heat of the day.

They're off and away with a rattle,
  Like dogs from the leashes let slip,
And right at the back of the battle
  He followed them under the whip.
They gained ten good lengths on him quickly,
  He dropped right away from the pack;
I tell you it made me feel sickly
  To see the blue jacket fall back.

Our very last hope had departed —
  We thought the old fellow was done,
When all of a sudden he started
  To go like a shot from a gun.
His chances seemed slight to embolden
  Our hearts; but, with teeth firmly set,
We thought, "Now or never! The old 'un
  May reckon with some of 'em yet."

Then loud rose the warcry for Pardon;
  He swept like the wind down the dip,
And over the rise by the garden,
  The jockey was done with the whip;
The field were at sixes and sevens —
  The pace at the first had been fast —
And hope seemed to drop from the heavens,
  For Pardon was coming at last.

And how he did come! It was splendid;
  He gained on them yards every bound,
Stretching out like a greyhound extended,
  His girth laid right down on the ground.
A shimmer of silk in the cedars
  As into the running they wheeled,
And out flashed the whips on the leaders,
  For Pardon had collared the field.

Then right through the ruck he came sailing —
  I knew that the battle was won —
The son of Haphazard was failing,
  The Yattendon filly was done;
He cut down the Don and the Dancer,
  He raced clean away from the mare —
He's in front! Catch him now if you can, sir!
  And up went my hat in the air!

Old Pardon, the Son of Reprieve

Then loud from the lawn and the garden
    Rose offers of "Ten to one *on!*"
"Who'll bet on the field? I back Pardon!"
    No use; all the money was gone.
He came for the third heat light-hearted,
    A-jumping and dancing about;
The others were done ere they started,
    Crestfallen, and tired, and worn out.

He won it, and ran it much faster
    Than even the first, I believe.
Oh, he was the daddy, the master,
    Was Pardon, the son of Reprieve.
He showed 'em the method to travel —
    The boy sat as still as a stone —
They never could see him for gravel;
    He came in hard-held, and alone.

But he's old — and his eyes are grown hollow;
    Like me, with my thatch of the snow;
When he dies, then I hope I may follow,
    And go where the racehorses go,
I don't want no harping nor singing —
    Such things with my style don't agree;
Where the hoofs of the horses are ringing
    There's music sufficient for me.

And surely the thoroughbred horses
    Will rise up again and begin
Fresh races on faraway courses
    And p'raps they might let me slip in.
It would look rather well the race card on
    'Mongst cherubs and seraphs and things,
"Angel Harrison's black gelding Pardon,
    Blue halo, white body and wings".

And if they have racing hereafter,
    (And who is to say they will not?)
When the cheers and the shouting and laughter
    Proclaim that the battle grows hot;
As they come down the racecourse a-steering,
    He'll rush to the front, I believe;
And you'll hear the great multitude cheering
    For Pardon, the son of Reprieve.

Pioneers

They came of bold and roving stock that would not fixed abide;
   They were the sons of field and flock since e'er they learned to ride;
We may not hope to see such men in these degenerate years
As those explorers of the bush — the brave old pioneers.

'Twas they who rode the trackless bush in heat and storm and drought;
'Twas they that heard the master-word that called them further out;
'Twas they that followed up the trail the mountain cattle made
And pressed across the mighty range where now their bones are laid.

But now the times are dull and slow, the brave old days are dead
When hardy bushmen started out, and forced their way ahead
By tangled scrub and forests grim towards the unknown west,
And spied the far-off promised land from off the ranges' crest.

Oh! ye, that sleep in lonely graves by far-off ridge and plain,
We drink to you in silence now as Christmas comes again,
The men who fought the wilderness through rough, unsettled years —
The founders of our nation's life, the brave old pioneers.

His Masterpiece

"GREENHIDE BILLY" was a stockman on a Clarence River cattle station and admittedly the biggest liar in the district. He had been for many years pioneering in the Northern Territory, the other side of the sundown — a regular "furthest-out man" — and this assured his reputation among station hands who award rank according to amount of experience. Young men who have always hung around the home localities, doing a job of shearing here or a turn at horse breaking there, look with reverence on the Riverine or Macquarie River shearers who come in with tales of runs where they have 300,000 acres of freehold land and shear 250,000 sheep, and these again pale their ineffectual fires before the glory of the Northern Territory man who has all comers on toast, because no one can contradict him or check his figures, except someone from the same locality. When two such meet, however, they are not fools enough to cut down quotations and spoil the market; no, they mutually lie in support of each other, and make all other bushmen feel mean and pitiful and inexperienced.

Sometimes a youngster would timidly ask Greenhide Billy about the (to him) *terra incognita*: "What sort of a place is it, Billy — how big are the properties? How many acres had you in the place you were on?"

"Acres be d——d!" Billy would scornfully reply, "hear him talking about acres! D'ye think we were blanked cockatoo selectors? Out there we reckon country by the hundred miles. You orter say, 'How many thousand miles of country?' and then I'd understand you."

Furthermore, according to Billy, they reckoned the rainfall in the Territory by yards, not inches; he had seen blackfellows who could jump at least three inches higher than anyone else had ever seen a blackfellow jump, and every bushman has seen or personally known a blackfellow who could jump over six feet. Billy had seen bigger droughts, better country, fatter cattle, faster horses, and cleverer dogs than any other man on the Clarence River. But one night when the rain was on the roof, and the river was rising with a moaning sound, and the men were gathered round the fire in the hut smoking and staring at the coals, Billy turned himself loose and gave us his masterpiece.

"I was drovin' with cattle from Mungrybanbone to old Corlett's station on the Buckatowndown River." (Billy always started his stories with some paralysing bush names.) "We had a thousand head of store cattle, wild mountain-bred wretches, they'd charge you on sight, and they were that handy with their horns they could skewer a mosquito. There was one or two one-eyed cattle among 'em, and you know how a one-eyed beast always keeps movin' away from the mob, pokin' away out to the edge of them so as they won't git on his blind side; and then by stirrin' about he keeps the others restless. They had been scared once or twice and stamped, and gave us all we could do to keep them together; and it was wet and dark and thundering, and it looked like a real bad night for us. It was my watch, and I was on one side of the cattle, like it might be here, with a small bit of a fire; and my mate, Barcoo Jim, he was right opposite on the other side of the cattle, and he had gone to sleep under a log. The rest of the men were in the camp fast asleep. Every now and again I'd get on my horse and prowl round the cattle quiet like, and they seemed to be settled down all right, and I was sitting by my fire holding my horse and drowsing, when all of a sudden a blessed possum ran out from some saplings and scratched up a little tree right alongside me. I was half asleep I suppose, and was startled; anyhow, never thinking what I was doing, I picked up a firestick out of the fire and flung it at the possum. Whoop! Before you could say 'Jack Robertson' that thousand head of cattle were on their feet, and they made one wild, headlong, mad rush right over the place where poor old Barcoo Jim was sleeping. There was no time to hunt up materials for the inquest; I had to keep those cattle together, so I sprang into the saddle, dashed the spurs into the old horse, dropped my head on his mane, and sent him as hard as he could leg it through the scrub to get the lead of the cattle and steady them. It was brigalow, and you know what that is. You know how the brigalow grows," continued Bill, "saplings about as thick as a man's arm, and that close together a dog can't open his mouth to bark in 'em. Well, those cattle swept through that scrub levelling it like as if it had been cleared for a railway line. They cleared a track a quarter of a mile wide, and smashed every stick, stump, and sapling on it. You could hear them roaring and their hoofs thundering and the scrub smashing three or four miles off. And where was I? I was racing parallel with the cattle with my head down on the horse's neck, letting him pick his way through the scrub in the pitchy darkness. This went on for about four miles, then the cattle began to get winded, and I dug into the old stock horse with the spurs, and got in front, and then began to crack the whip and sing out, so as to steady them a little; after a while they dropped slower and slower, and I kept the whip going. I got them all together in a patch of open country, and there I rode round and round 'em all night till daylight. And how I wasn't killed in the scrub, goodness only knows; for a man couldn't ride in the daylight where I did in the dark. The cattle were all knocked about — horns smashed, legs broken, ribs torn; but they were all there, every solitary head of 'em; and as soon as the daylight broke I took 'em back to the camp — that is, all that could travel, because a few broken-legged ones I had to leave.''

Billy paused in his narrative. He knew that some suggestions would be made, by way of compromise, to tone down the awful strength of the yarn, and he prepared himself accordingly. His motto was, ''No surrender''; he never abated one jot of his statements, and if anyone chose to remark on them, he made them warmer and stronger, and absolutely flattened out the intruder.

''That was a wonderful bit of ridin' you done, Billy,'' said one of the men at last, admiringly. ''It's a wonder you wasn't killed. I s'pose your clothes was pretty well tore off your back with the scrub?''

''Never touched a twig,'' said Billy.

''Ah!'' faltered the enquirer, ''then no doubt you had a real ringin' good stock horse that could take you through a scrub like that full split in the dark, and not hit you against anything.''

''No, he wasn't a good 'un,'' said Billy decisively, ''he was the worst horse in the camp, and terrible awkward in the scrub he was, always fallin' down on his knees; and his neck was so short you could sit far back on him and pull his ears.''

Here that interrogator retired hurt; he gave Billy best. Another took up the running after a pause.

''How did your mate get on, Billy? I s'pose he was trampled to a mummy!''

''No,'' said Billy, ''he wasn't hurt a bit. I told you he was sleeping under the shelter of a little log. Well, when these cattle rushed they swept over that log a thousand strong; and every beast of that herd took the log in his stride and just missed landing on Barcoo Jimmy by about four inches. We saw the tracks where they had cleared him in the night — and fancy that, a thousand head of cattle to charge over a man in the dark and just miss him by a hair's breadth, as you might say!''

The men waited a while and smoked, to let this statement soak well into their systems; at last one rallied and had a final try to get a suggestion in somewhere.

''It's a wonder, then, Billy,'' he said, ''that your mate didn't come after you and give you a hand to steady the cattle.''

''Well, perhaps it was,'' said Billy, ''only that there was a bigger wonder than that at the back of it.''

''What was that?''

''My mate never woke all through it.''

Then the men knocked the ashes out of their pipes and went to bed.

Buffalo Country

Out where the grey streams glide,
  Sullen and deep and slow,
And the alligators slide
From the mud to the depths below
Or drift on the stream like a floating death,
Where the fever comes on the south wind's breath,
There is the buffalo.

Out on the big lagoons,
Where the Regia lilies float,
And the Nankin heron croons
With a deep ill-omened note,
In the ooze and the mud of the swamps below
Lazily wallows the buffalo,
Buried to nose and throat.

From the hunter's gun he hides
In the jungles dark and damp,
Where the slinking dingo glides
And the flying foxes camp;
Hanging like myriad fiends in line
Where the trailing creepers twist and twine
And the sun is a sluggish lamp.

On the edge of the rolling plains
Where the coarse cane grasses swell,
Lush with the tropic rains
In the noontide's drowsy spell,
Slowly the buffalo grazes through
Where the brolgas dance, and the jabiru
Stands like a sentinel.

All that the world can know
Of the wild and the weird is here,
Where the black men come and go
With their boomerang and spear,
And the wild duck darken the evening sky
As they fly to their nests in the reed beds high
When the tropic night is near.

Campin' Round Coonamble

Campin' round Coonamble,
    Keepin' up the strike,
Through the black soil country
    Plugging on the ''bike'';
Half a thousand shearers,
    What had we to gain
Campin' round Coonamble,
    Campin' in the rain?

Twenty bob a hundred
    Shearing with machines!
Good enough in these times
    We know what it means —
Sinking tanks and fencing,
    Shearing's better pay,
Twenty bob a hundred,
    Twenty bob a day!

Every little farmer
    Up Monaro side
Sends the boys a-shearing,
    Hoping to provide
Something for the homestead;
    All his hopes are vain,
While we're round Coonamble,
    Campin' in the rain.

Up at old man Tobin's,
    First pen on the right,
Don't I know his wethers,
    Know 'em all by sight!
Many a year I shore 'em
    Like to shear again,
Better game than campin',
    Campin' in the rain.

What's the use of talking
  Five-and-twenty bob,
While there's hundreds hungry
  Looking for a job?
Darling Harbour casuals,
  Hollow in the cheek,
Cadging from the Government
  Two days' work a week.

When with peal of trumpets,
  And with beat of drums,
Labour's great millennium
  Actually comes;
When each white Australian,
  Master of his craft,
Keeps a foreign servant
  Just to do the graft;

When the price of shearing
  Goes to fifty bob,
And there's no man hungry
  Looking for a job;
Then, if they oppress us,
  Then we'll go again
Campin' round Coonamble,
  Campin' in the rain.

The Travelling Post Office

The roving breezes come and go, the reed beds sweep and sway,
  The sleepy river murmurs low, and loiters on its way,
It is the land of lots o' time along the Castlereagh.

The old man's son had left the farm, he found it dull and slow,
He drifted to the great north-west where all the rovers go.
"He's gone so long," the old man said, "he's dropped right out of mind,
But if you'd write a line to him I'd take it very kind;
He's shearing here and fencing there, a kind of waif and stray,
He's droving now with Conroy's sheep along the Castlereagh.
The sheep are travelling for the grass, and travelling very slow;
They may be at Mundooran now, or past the Overflow,
Or tramping down the black soil flats across by Waddiwong,
But all those little country towns would send the letter wrong.
The mailman, if he's extra tired, would pass them in his sleep,
It's safest to address the note to 'Care of Conroy's sheep',
For five and twenty thousand head can scarcely go astray,
You write to 'Care of Conroy's sheep along the Castlereagh'."

By rock and ridge and riverside the western mail has gone,
Across the great Blue Mountain Range to take that letter on.
A moment on the topmost grade while open fire doors glare,
She pauses like a living thing to breathe the mountain air,
Then launches down the other side across the plains away
To bear that note to "Conroy's sheep along the Castlereagh".

And now by coach and mailman's bag it goes from town to town,
And Conroy's Gap and Conroy's Creek have marked it "further down".
Beneath a sky of deepest blue where never cloud abides,
A speck upon the waste of plain the lonely mailman rides.
Where fierce hot winds have set the pine and myall boughs asweep
He hails the shearers passing by for news of Conroy's sheep.
By big lagoons where wildfowl play and crested pigeons flock,
By campfires where the drovers ride around their restless stock,
And past the teamster toiling down to fetch the wool away
My letter chases Conroy's sheep along the Castlereagh.

The Travelling Post Office

A speck upon the waste of plain the lonely mailman rides.   page 48

Waltzing Matilda

Up came the squatter a-riding his thoroughbred;
Up came policemen — one, two, and three. page 49

Waltzing Matilda

Oh there once was a swagman camped in the billabongs,
  Under the shade of a Coolibah tree;
And he sang as he looked at the old billy boiling,
  "Who'll come a-waltzing Matilda with me."

Who'll come a-waltzing Matilda, my darling,
  Who'll come a-waltzing Matilda with me.
Waltzing Matilda and leading a water-bag,
  Who'll come a-waltzing Matilda with me.

Up came the jumbuck to drink at the waterhole,
  Up jumped the swagman and grabbed him in glee;
And he sang as he put him away in his tucker-bag,
  "You'll come a-waltzing Matilda with me!"

Who'll come a-waltzing Matilda, my darling,
  Who'll come a-waltzing Matilda with me.
Waltzing Matilda and leading a water-bag,
  Who'll come a-waltzing Matilda with me.

Up came the squatter a-riding his thoroughbred;
  Up came policemen — one, two, and three.
"Whose is the jumbuck you've got in the tucker-bag?
  You'll come a-waltzing Matilda with we."

Who'll come a-waltzing Matilda, my darling,
  Who'll come a-waltzing Matilda with me?
Waltzing Matilda and leading a water-bag,
  Who'll come a-waltzing Matilda with me.

Up sprang the swagman and jumped in the waterhole,
  Drowning himself by the Coolibah tree;
And his voice can be heard as it sings in the billabongs,
  "Who'll come a-waltzing Matilda with me."

Who'll come a-waltzing Matilda, my darling,
  Who'll come a-waltzing Matilda with me.
Waltzing Matilda and leading a water-bag,
  Who'll come a-waltzing Matilda with me.

Three Elephant Power

"THEM THINGS", said Alfred the chauffeur, tapping the speed indicator with his finger, "them things are all right for the police. But, Lord, you can fix 'em up if you want to. Did you ever hear about Henery, that used to drive for old John Bull — Henery and the ellyphunt?"

Alfred was chauffeur to a friend of mine, a friend who owned a very powerful car, and Alfred was part of the car. He was an Australian youth. It is strange that in Australia the motor has already produced the motor type. Weirdly intelligent, of poor physique, Alfred might have been any age from fifteen to eighty. His education had been somewhat hurried, but there was no doubt as to his mechanical ability. He took to a car like a young duck to water. He talked motor, and thought motor, and would have accepted with — well, I won't say enthusiasm, for Alfred's motto was *Nil admirari* — but without hesitation, an offer to drive in the greatest race in the world. He could drive really well, too, and as for belief in himself, after six months' apprenticeship in a garage, he was prepared to vivisect a six-cylinder engine with the confidence of a diplomaed Bachelor of Engineering.

Barring a tendency to flash driving and a delight in "persecuting" slow cars by driving just in front of them and letting them come up and enjoy his dust, and then shooting away again, he was a very respectable member of society. When his "boss" was in the car he cloaked the natural ferocity of his instincts; but this day, with only myself as passenger on board, and a clear run of 120 miles up to the station before him, he let her loose, confident that if any trouble occurred I would be held morally responsible.

As we fled past a somnolent bush public house, Alfred, whistling softly, leant forward and turned on a little more oil.

"You never heard about Henery and the ellyphunt?" he said. "It was dead funny. Henery was a bushwacker, but clean mad on motorin'. He was wood and water joey at some squatter's place, you know, and he seen a motor car go past one day, the first that ever they had in the districk. 'That's my game,' says Henery; 'no more wood and water joey

50

for me.' So he comes to town and gets a job off Miles that had that garage at the back of Allison's. And an old cove that they call John Bull — I don't know his right name, he was a fat old cove — he used to come there to hire cars, and Henery used to drive him. And this old John Bull he had lots of stuff, so at last he reckons he's going to get a car for himself, and he promises Henery a job to drive it. A queer cove this Henery was — half mad, I think — but the best hand with a car ever I see.''

While he had been talking we topped a hill and opened up a new stretch of blue-grey granite-like road. Down at the foot of the hill before us was a teamster's waggon in camp: the horses in their harness munching at their nose bags, while the teamster and a mate were boiling a billy a little off to the side of the road. There was a turn in the road just below the waggon which looked a bit sharp, so of course Alfred bore down on it like a whirlwind. The big stupid team horses huddled together and pushed each other awkwardly as we passed. A dog that had been sleeping in the shade of the waggon sprang out from beneath it right in front of the car, and was exterminated without ever knowing what struck him. There was just room to clear the tail of the waggon to negotiate the turn, and as Alfred, with the calm decision of a Napoleon, swung round the bend, he found that the old teamster's hack, fast asleep, was tied to the tail of the waggon, and nothing but a most lightning-like twist of the steering wheel prevented our scooping the old animal up, and taking him on board as a passenger. As it was, we got a lot of his tail as a trophy caught on the brass of the lamp. The old steed, thus rudely awakened, lashed out good and hard, but by the time he kicked we were gone and he missed the car by a quarter of a mile. During this strenuous episode, Alfred never relaxed his professional stolidity, and when we were clear he went on with his story in the tone of a man who found life wanting in animation.

''Well, at fust, the old man would only buy one of these little eight-horse rubby dubbys that used to go strugglin' up the 'ills with the death rattle in its throat, and all the people in buggies passin' it. And o' course that didn't suit Henery. He used to get that spiked when a car passed him he'd nearly go mad. And one day he nearly got the sack for dodging his car about up a steep 'ill in front of one o' them big twenty-four Darracqs, full of 'owlin' toffs, and wouldn't let 'em get a chance to go past till they got to the top of the 'ill. But at last he persuaded old John Bull to let him go to England and buy a car for him. He was to do a year in the shops, and pick up all the wrinkles and get a car for the old man. Bit better than wood and water joeying, wasn't it?''

Our progress here was barred by our rounding a corner right onto a flock of sheep, that at once packed together into a solid mass in front of us, blocking the whole road from fence to fence. ''Silly cows o' things, ain't they?'' said Alfred, putting on his emergency brake, and skidding up till the car softly came to rest against the cushion-like mass

— a much quicker stop than any horse-drawn vehicle could have made in the time. A few sheep were crushed somewhat, but it is well known that a sheep is practically indestructible by violence. Whatever Alfred's faults were, he could certainly drive.

"Well," he went on, lighting a cigarette, unheeding the growls of the drovers, who were trying to get the sheep to pass the car, "well, as I was sayin', Henery went to England, and he got a car. Do you know wot he got?"

"No, I don't."

" 'E got a ninety," said Alfred, giving time for the words to soak in.

"A ninety! What do you mean?"

" 'E got a ninety — a ninety-horse power racin' engine that was made for some American millionaire, and wasn't as fast as wot some other millionaire had, so he sold it for the price of the iron, and Henery got it, and had a body built for it, and he come out here, and tells us all it's a twenty mongrel — you know, one of them cars that's made part in one place and part in another, the body here and the engine there, and the radiator another place. There's lots of cheap cars made like that. So Henery he says that this is a twenty mongrel — only a four-cylinder engine — and nobody drops to what she is till Henery goes out one Sunday and waits for the big Napier that Scotty used to drive — it belonged to the same bloke that owned that big racehorse what won all the races. So Henery and Scotty they have a fair go round the park while both their bosses is at church, and Henery beat him out o' sight — fair lost him — and so Henery was reckoned the boss of the road. No one would take him on after that."

A nasty creek crossing here required all Alfred's attention. A little girl, carrying a billy can of water, stood by the stepping stones, and smiled shyly as we passed, and Alfred waved her a salute quite as though he were an ordinary human being. I felt comforted. He had his moments of relaxation, evidently, and his affections the same as other people.

"And what happened to Henery and the ninety-horse machine?" I said. "Where does the elephant come in? For a chauffeur, you're a long time coming to the elephant."

Alfred smiled pityingly.

"Ain't I tellin' yer?" he said. "You wouldn't understand if I didn't tell yer how he got the car and all that. So here's Henery," he went on, "with old John Bull goin' about in the fastest car in Australia, and old John, he's a quiet old geezer, that wouldn't drive faster than the regulations for anything, and he's that short-sighted he can't see to the side of the road. So what does Henery do, but he fixes the speed indicator — puts a new face on it, so that when the car is doing thirty, the indicator only shows fifteen, and twenty for forty and so on. So out they'd go and if Henery knew there was a big car in front of him, he'd let out to forty-five, and the pace would very near blow the whiskers off old John, and every now and again he'd look at the indicator, and it'd be showin' twenty-two and a half, and he'd say, 'Better be careful, Henery, you're slightly exceedin' the speed limit; twenty miles an hour, you know, Henery, should be fast enough for anybody, and you're doing over twenty-two.' And one day, Henery told me he was tryin' to catch up a big car that just came out from France, and it had a half-hour start of him, and he was just fairly flyin', an' there was a lot of cars on the road, and he flies past 'em so fast the old man says, 'It's very strange, Henery,' he says, 'that all the cars that are out to-day are comin' this way,' he says. You see he was passin' 'em so fast he thought they were all comin' towards him. And Henery sees a mate of his coming, so he lets out a notch or two, and the two cars flew by each other like chain lightnin'. They were each doin' about forty, and the old man, he says, 'There's a driver must be travellin' a hundred miles an hour,' he says, 'I never see a car go by so fast in my life,' he says. 'If I could find out who he is, I'd report him,' he says. 'Did you know the car, Henery?' But of course Henery, he doesn't know, so on they goes. And when they caught the French car — the owner of it thinks he has the fastest car in Australia — and Henery and the old man are seen coming, he tells his driver to let her out a little, but Henery gives the ninety-horse the full of the lever, and whips up alongside in one jump. And then he keeps there just half a length ahead of him, tormentin' him, like. And the owner of the French car he yowls out to old John Bull, 'You're goin' a nice pace for an old 'un,' he says. Old John has a blink down at the indicator. 'We're doing twenty-five,' he yells out. 'Twenty-five grandmothers,' says the bloke; but Henery put on his accelerator and left him. It wouldn't do to let the old man get wise to it, you know.''

We topped a big hill, and Alfred cut off the engine and let the car swoop as swiftly and as noiselessly as an eagle down to the flat country below.

''You're a long while coming to the elephant, Alfred,'' I said.

''Well, now, I'll tell you about the ellyphunt,'' said Alfred, letting his clutch in again, and taking up the story to the accompaniment of the rhythmic throb of the engine. ''One day Henery and the old man were going a long trip over the mountain, and down the Kangaroo Valley road that's all cut out of the side of the 'ill. And after they's gone a mile or two, Henery sees a track in the road — the track of the biggest car he ever saw or heard of. An' the more he looks at it, the more he reckons he must ketch that car and see what's she made of. So he slows down, passin' two yokels on the road, and he says, 'Did you see a big car along 'ere?' 'Yes, we did,' they says. 'How big is she?' says Henery. 'Biggest car ever we see,' says the yokels, and they laughed that silly way these yokels always does.

'' 'How many horsepower do you think she was?' says Henery.

" 'Horse power,' they says; 'elephant power you mean! she was three elephant power!' they says; and they goes, 'Haw, haw' and Henery drops his clutch in, and off he goes after that car."

Alfred lit another cigarette as a preliminary to the climax.

"So they run for miles, and all the time there's the track ahead of 'em, and Henery keeps lettin' her out, thinkin' that he'll never ketch that car. They went through a town so fast, the old man he says, 'What house was that we just passed?' he says. So at last they come to the top of the big 'ill, and there's the tracks of the big car goin' straight down ahead of 'em. D'you know that road? It's all cut out of the side of the mountain, and there's places where if she was to side-slip you'd go down 'undreds of thousands of feet. And there's sharp turns, too, but the surface is good, so Henery he lets her out, and down they go, whizzin' round the turns and skatin' out near the edge, and the old cove sittin' there enjoyin' it, never knowin' the danger. And comin' to one turn Henery gives a toot on the 'orn, and then he heard somethin' go 'Toot, toot' right away down the mountain. 'Bout a mile ahead it seemed to be, and Henery reckoned he'd go another four miles before he'd ketch it, so he chances them turns more than ever. And she was pretty hot, too; but he kept her at it, and he hadn't gone a full mile till he come round a turn about forty miles an hour, and before he could stop he run right into it, and wot do you think it was?"

I hadn't the faintest idea.

"A circus. One of them travellin' circuses, goin' down the coast, and one of the ellyphunts had sore feet, so they put him in a big waggon and another ellyphunt pulled in front and one pushed behind. Three ellyphunt power it was, right enough. That was the waggon that made the big track. Well, it was all done so sudden. Before Henery could stop, he runs the radiator — very near boiling she was — up against the ellyphunt's tail, and prints the pattern of the latest honeycomb radiator on the ellyphunt as clear as if you done it with a stencil plate. And the ellyphunt, he lets a roar out of him like one of them bulls bellerin', and he puts out his nose and ketches Henery round the neck, and yanks him out of the car, and chucks him right clean over the cliff, 'bout a thousand feet. But he never done nothin' to the old bloke."

"Good gracious!"

"Well, it finished Henery, killed him stone dead, of course, and the old man he was terrible cut up over losin' such a steady, trustworthy man. Never get another like him, he says."

We were nearly at our journey's end, and we turned through a gate into the home paddocks. Some young stock, both horses and cattle, came frisking and cantering after the car, and the rough bush track took all Alfred's attention. We crossed a creek, the water swishing from the wheels, and began the long pull up to the homestead. Over the clamour of the little-used second speed, Alfred concluded his narrative.

"The old bloke advertised," he said, "for another driver, a steady reliable man to drive a twenty-horse power, four-cylinder touring car. An' every driver in Sydney put in for it. Nothing like a fast car to fetch 'em, you know. And Scotty got it. Him that used to drive the Napier I was tellin' you about.''

''And what did the old man say when he found he'd been running a racing car?''

''He don't know now. Scotty never told 'im. Why should he? He's drivin' about the country now, the boss of the roads, but he won't chance her near a circus. Thinks he might bump the same ellyphunt. And they reckon that ellyphunt, when he's in the circus, every time he smells a car passin' in the road, he goes near mad with fright. If he ever sees that car again, do you think he'd know it?''

Not being used to the capacities of elephants, I could not offer an opinion.

Been There Before

There came a stranger to Walgett town,
   To Walgett town when the sun was low,
And he carried a thirst that was worth a crown,
   Yet how to quench it he did not know;
But he thought he might take those yokels down,
The guileless yokels of Walgett town.

They made him a bet in a private bar,
   In a private bar when the talk was high,
And they bet him some pounds no matter how far
   He could pelt a stone, yet he could not shy
A stone right over the river so brown,
The Darling River at Walgett town.

He knew that the river from bank to bank
   Was fifty yards, and he smiled a smile
As he trundled down, but his hopes they sank
   For there wasn't a stone within fifty mile;
For the saltbush plain and the open down
Produce no quarries in Walgett town.

The yokels laughed at his hopes o'erthrown,
   And he stood awhile like a man in a dream;
Then out of his pocket he fetched a stone,
   And pelted it over the silent stream —
He had been there before: he had wandered down
On a previous visit to Walgett town.

Been There Before

Then out of his pocket he fetched a stone   page 56

Three Elephant Power

". . . Before Henery could stop, he runs the radiator — very near boiling she was — up against the ellyphunt's tail . . ."

Fur and Feathers

So down the ground like fire he fled
And leaped above an emu's head   page 57

Fur and Feathers

The emus formed a football team
    Up Walgett way;
Their dark-brown sweaters were a dream
But kangaroos would sit and scream
    To watch them play.

"Now, butterfingers," they would call,
    And such-like names;
The emus couldn't hold the ball
— They had no hands — but hands aren't all
    In football games.

A match against the kangaroos
    They played one day.
The kangaroos were forced to choose
Some wallabies and wallaroos
    That played in grey.

The rules that in the west prevail
    Would shock the town;
For when a kangaroo set sail
An emu jumped upon his tail
    And fetched him down.

A whistler duck as referee
    Was not admired.
He whistled so incessantly
The teams rebelled, and up a tree
    He soon retired.

The old marsupial captain said,
    "It's do or die!"
So down the ground like fire he fled
And leaped above an emu's head
    And scored a try.

Then shouting, ''Keep it on the toes!''
    The emus came.
Fierce as the flooded Bogan flows
They laid their foemen out in rows
    And saved the game.

On native pear and Darling pea
    They dined that night:
But one man was an absentee:
The whistler duck — their referee —
    Had taken flight.

The Merino Sheep

THE PROSPERITY OF Australia is absolutely based on a beast — the merino sheep. If all the sheep in the country were to die, the big banks would collapse like card houses, the squatting securities, which are their backbone, being gone. Business would perish, and the money we owe to England would be as hopelessly lost to that nation as if we were a South American state. The sheep, and the sheep alone, keeps us going. On the back of this beneficent creature we all live. Knowing this, people have got the impression that the merino sheep is a gentle, bleating animal that gets its living without trouble to anybody, and comes up every year to be shorn with a pleased smile upon its amiable face. It is my purpose here, as one having experience, to exhibit the merino sheep in its true light, so that the public may know what kind of brute they are depending on.

And first let us give him what little credit is his due. No one can accuse him of being a ferocious animal. No one could ever say that a sheep attacked him without provocation, though there is an old bush story of a man who was discovered in the act of killing a neighbour's wether. "Hullo," said the neighbour. "What's this? Killing my sheep! What have you got to say for yourself?" "Yes," said the man, with an air of virtuous indignation. "I *am* killing your sheep. I'll kill *any* man's sheep that bites *me*!" But as a rule the merino refrains from using his teeth on people, and goes to work in another way.

The truth is that the merino sheep is a dangerous monomaniac, and his one idea is to ruin the man who owns him. With this object in view, he will display a talent for getting into trouble and a genius for dying that are almost incredible. If a mob of sheep see a bushfire closing round them, do they run away out of danger? Not at all; they rush round and round in a ring till the fire burns them up. If they are in a river bed, with a howling flood coming down, they will stubbornly refuse to cross three inches of water to save themselves. Dogs and men may bark and shriek, but the sheep won't move. They will wait there till the flood comes and drowns them all, and then their corpses go down the river on their backs with their feet in the air. A mob of sheep will crawl along a road slowly enough to exasperate a snail, but let a lamb get away from

59

the mob in a bit of rough country, and a racehorse can't head him back again. If sheep are put into a big paddock with water in three corners of it, they will resolutely crowd into the fourth corner and die of thirst. When sheep are being counted out at a gate, if a scrap of bark be left on the ground in the gateway, they will refuse to step over it until dogs and men have sweated and toiled and sworn and "heeled 'em up", and "spoke to 'em", and fairly jammed them at it. Then the first one will gather courage, rush at the fancied obstacle, spring over it about six feet in the air and dart away. The next does exactly the same, but jumps a bit higher. Then comes a rush of them following one another in wild bounds like antelopes, until one "over-jumps himself" and alights on his head, a performance which nothing but a sheep could compass.

This frightens those still in the yard, and they stop running out, and the dogging and shrieking and hustling and tearing have to be gone through all over again. This on a red-hot day, mind you, with clouds of blinding dust about, with the yolk of wool irritating your eyes, and with, perhaps, three or four thousand sheep to put through. The delay throws out the man who is counting, and he forgets whether he left off at 45 or 95. The dogs, meanwhile, take the first chance to slip over the fence and hide in the shade somewhere. Then there are loud whistlings and oaths, and calls for Rover and Bluey, and at last a dirt-begrimed man jumps over the fence, unearths a dog and hauls him back to work by the ear. The dog sets to barking and heeling 'em up again, and pretends that he thoroughly enjoys it, but he is looking out all the time for another chance to "clear". And *this* time he won't be discovered in a hurry.

To return to our muttons. There is a well-authenticated story of a shipload of sheep being lost once, because an old ram jumped overboard into the ocean, and all the rest followed him. No doubt they did, and were proud to do it. A sheep won't go through an open gate on his own responsibility, but he would gladly and proudly follow another sheep through the red-hot portals of Hades: and it makes no difference whether the leader goes voluntarily or is hauled struggling and kicking and fighting every inch of the way. For pure, sodden stupidity there is no animal like the merino sheep. A lamb will follow a bullock dray drawn by sixteen bullocks and driven by a profane "colonial" with a whip, under the impression that this aggregate monstrosity is his mother. A ewe never knows her own lamb by sight, and apparently has no sense of colour. She can recognise her own lamb's voice half a mile off among a thousand other voices apparently exactly similar, but when she gets within five yards of her lamb she starts to smell all the lambs in reach, including the black ones, though her own may be a white lamb. The fiendish resemblance which one sheep bears to another is a great advantage to them in their struggles with their owners. It makes them more difficult to draft out of a strange flock, and much harder to tell when any are missing.

Concerning this resemblance between sheep, there is a story told of a fat old Murrumbidgee squatter who gave a big price for a famous ram called, say, Sir Oliver. He took a friend out one day to inspect Sir Oliver, and overhauled that animal with a most impressive air of sheep wisdom. "Look here," he said, "at the fineness of the wool. See the serrations in each thread of it. See the density of it. Look at the way his legs and belly are clothed — he's wool all over, that sheep. Grand animal, grand animal!" Then they went and had a drink, and the old squatter said, "Now, I'll show you the difference between a champion ram and a second-rater". So he caught a ram and pointed out his defects. "See here — not half the serrations that other sheep had. No density of fleece to speak of. Bare-bellied as a pig, compared with Sir Oliver. Not that this isn't a fair sheep, but he'd be dear at one-tenth Sir Oliver's price. By the way, Johnson" (to his overseer) "what ram *is* this?" "That, sir," replied the astounded functionary, "that's Sir Oliver, sir!" And so it was.

There is another kind of sheep in Australia, as great a curse in his own way as the merino — namely, the cross-bred or half-merino-half-Leicester animal. The cross-bred will get through, under or over any fence you like to put in front of him. He is never satisfied on his owner's run, but always thinks other people's runs must be better, so he sets off to explore. He will strike a course, say, south-east, and so long as the fit takes him he will keep going south-east through all obstacles, rivers, fences, growing crops — anything. The merino relies on passive resistance for his success; the cross-bred carries the war into the enemy's camp, and becomes a living curse to his owner day and night. Once there was a man who was induced in a weak moment to buy twenty cross-bred rams, and from that hour the hand of fate was upon him. They got into all the paddocks they shouldn't have been in. They scattered themselves all over the run promiscuously. They got into the cultivation paddock and the vegetable garden at their own sweet will. And then they took to roving. In a body they visited the neighbouring stations, and played havoc with the sheep all over the district. The wretched owner was constantly getting fiery letters from his neighbours: "Your — rams are here. Come and take them away at once", and he would have to go off nine or ten miles to drive them home. Any man who has tried to drive rams on a hot day knows what purgatory is. He was threatened with actions for trespass for scores of pounds damages every week. He tried shutting them up in the sheep yard. They got out and went back to the garden. Then he gaoled them in the calf pen. Out again and into a growing crop. Then he set a boy to watch them, but the boy went to sleep, and they were four miles away across country before he got on to their tracks. At length, when they happened accidentally to be at home on their owner's run, there came a huge flood. His sheep, mostly merinos, had plenty of time to get on to high ground and save their lives, but, of course, they didn't, and they were almost all drowned. The owner sat on a rise above the waste of waters and watched the dead animals go by. He was a ruined man. His hopes in life were gone. But he said, ''Thank God, those rams are drowned, anyhow.'' Just as he spoke there was a splashing in the water, and the twenty rams solemnly swam ashore and ranged themselves in front of him. They were the only survivors of thousands of sheep. He broke down utterly, and was taken to an asylum for insane paupers. The cross-breds had fulfilled their destiny.

The cross-bred drives his owner out of his mind, but the merino ruins his man with greater celerity. Nothing on earth will kill cross-breds, while nothing will keep merinos alive. If they are put on dry saltbush country they die of drought. If they are put on damp, well-watered country they die of worms, fluke, and foot rot. They die in the wet seasons and they die in the dry ones. The hard, resentful look which you may notice on the faces of all bushmen comes from a long course of dealing with the merino sheep. It is the merino sheep which dominates the bush, and which gives to Australian literature its melancholy tinge, and its despairing pathos. The poems about dying boundary riders and lonely graves under mournful she-oaks are the direct outcome of the author's too close association with that soul-destroying animal, the merino sheep. A man who could write anything cheerful after a day in the drafting yards would be a freak of nature.

The Amateur Rider

Him going to ride for us! *Him* — with the pants and the eyeglass
   and all.
Amateur! don't he just look it — it's twenty to one on a fall.
Boss must be gone off his head to be sending our steeplechase crack
Out over fences like these with an object like that on his back.

Ride! Don't tell *me* he can ride. With his pants just as loose as balloons,
How can he sit on his horse? And his spurs like a pair of harpoons;
Ought to be under the Dog Act, he ought, and be kept off the course.
Fall! why, he'd fall off a cart, let alone off a steeplechase horse.

Yessir! the 'orse is all ready — I wish you'd have rode him before;
Nothing like knowing your 'orse, sir, and this chap's a terror to bore;
Battleaxe always could pull, and he rushes his fences like fun —
Stands off his jump twenty feet, and then springs like a shot from a gun.

Oh, he can jump 'em all right, sir, you make no mistake, 'e's a toff;
Clouts 'em in earnest, too, sometimes, you mind that he don't clout
    you off —
Don't seem to mind how he hits 'em, his shins is as hard as a nail,
Sometimes you'll see the fence shake and the splinters fly up from the
    rail.

All you can do is to hold him and just let him jump as he likes,
Give him his head at the fences, and hang on like death if he strikes;
Don't let him run himself out — you can lie third or fourth in the
    race —
Until you clear the stone wall, and from that you can put on the pace.

Fell at that wall once, he did, and it gave him a regular spread,
Ever since that time he flies it — he'll stop if you pull at his head,
Just let him race — you can trust him — he'll take first-class care he
    don't fall,
And I think that's the lot — but remember, *he must have his head at
    the wall.*

Well, he's down safe as far as the start, and he seems to sit on pretty
        neat,
Only his baggified breeches would ruinate anyone's seat —
They're away — here they come — the first fence, and he's head over
        heels for a crown!
Good for the new chum, he's over, and two of the others are down!

Now for the treble, my hearty — By Jove, he can ride, after all;
Whoop, that's your sort — let him fly them! He hasn't much fear of a
        fall.
Who in the world would have thought it? And aren't they just going a
        pace?
Little Recruit in the lead there will make it a stoutly run race.

Lord! But they're racing in earnest — and down goes Recruit on his
        head,
Rolling clean over his boy — it's a miracle if he ain't dead.
Battleaxe, Battleaxe yet! By the Lord, he's got most of 'em beat —
Ho! did you see how he struck, and the swell never moved in his seat?

Second time round, and, by Jingo! he's holding his lead of 'em well;
Hark to him clouting the timber! It don't seem to trouble the swell.
Now for the wall — let him rush it. A thirty-foot leap, I declare —
Never a shift in his seat, and he's racing for home like a hare.

What's that that's chasing him — Rataplan — regular demon to stay!
Sit down and ride for your life now! Oh, good, that's the style — come
        away!
Rataplan's certain to beat you, unless you can give him the slip;
Sit down and rub in the whalebone now — give him the spurs and the
        whip!

Battleaxe, Battleaxe, yet — and it's Battleaxe wins for a crown;
Look at him rushing the fences, he wants to bring t'other chap down.
Rataplan never will catch him if only he keeps on his pins;
Now! the last fence! and he's over it! Battleaxe, Battleaxe wins!

Well, sir, you rode him just perfect — I knew from the first you could
        ride.
Some of the chaps said you couldn't, an' I says just like this a' one side:
Mark me, I says, that's a tradesman — the saddle is where he was bred.
Weight! you're all right, sir, and thank you; and them was the words
        that I said.

The Amateur Rider

All you can do is to hold him and just let him jump as he likes   page 63

The Cat

"Isn't it sweet of him! Isn't he intelligent! He wants you to give him something to eat."

The Cat

FEW KNOW anything about domestic animals — about their inner life and the workings of their minds. Take, for instance, the common roof-tree cat. Most people think that the cat is an unintelligent animal, fond of ease, and caring little for anything but mice and milk. But a cat has really more character than most human beings, and gets a great deal more satisfaction out of life. Of all the animal kingdom, the cat has the most many-sided character. He — or she — is an athlete, a musician, an acrobat, a Lothario, a grim fighter, a sport of the first water. All day long, the cat loafs about the house and takes things easy, and sleeps by the fire, and allows himself to be pestered by the attentions of silly women and annoyed by children. To pass the time away he sometimes watches a mouse hole for an hour or two — just to keep himself from dying of ennui, and people get the idea that this sort of thing is all that life holds for the cat. But watch him as the shades of evening fall, and you see the cat as he really is.

When the family sits down to tea, the cat usually puts in an appearance to get his share, and he purrs noisily and rubs himself against the legs of the family, and all the time he is thinking of a fight or a love affair that is coming off that evening. If there is a guest at the table the cat is particularly civil to him, because the guest is likely to have the best of what food is going. Sometimes, instead of recognising his civility with something to eat, the guest stoops down and strokes the cat, and says, "Poor pussy! Poor pussy!" The cat soon gets tired of that — he puts up his claw and quietly but firmly rakes the guest in the leg.

"Ow!" says the guest, "the cat stuck his claw into me!" The family is delighted. It remarks, "Isn't it sweet of him? Isn't he intelligent? *He wants you to give him something to eat.*"

The guest dare not do what he would like to do — kick the cat through the window — so with tears of rage and pain in his eyes, he affects to be very much amused, and sorts out a bit of fish from his plate and gives it to the cat. The cat gingerly receives it, with a look in his eyes as much as to say: "Another time, my friend, you won't be so dull of comprehension," and purrs maliciously as he carries the bit of fish away to a safe distance from the guest's boot before eating it. A cat isn't a fool — not by a long way.

When the family has finished tea, and gathers round the fire to enjoy the hours of indigestion together, the cat slouches casually out of the room and disappears. Life, true life, now begins for him. He saunters down his own backyard, springs to the top of the fence with one easy bound, drops lightly down the other side, trots across a right-of-way to a vacant allotment, and skips to the roof of an empty shed. As he goes, he throws off the effeminate look of civilisation; his gait becomes lithe and panther-like; he looks quickly, keenly, from side to side, and moves noiselessly, for he has many enemies — dogs, cabmen with whips, and small boys with stones. Arrived on the top of the shed, the cat arches his back and rakes his claws once or twice through the soft bark of the old roof, then wheels round and stretches himself a few times, just to see that every muscle is in full working order; and then, dropping his head nearly to his paws, sends across a league of backyards his call to his kindred — his call to love, or war, or sport.

Before long they come — gliding, graceful shadows, approaching circuitously, and halting occasionally to look round and reconnoitre — tortoiseshell, tabby, and black, all domestic cats, but all transformed for the nonce into their natural state. No longer are they the hypocritical, meek creatures who an hour ago were cadging for fish and milk. They are now ruffling, swaggering blades with a Gascon sense of their dignity. Their fights are grim, determined battles, and a cat will be clawed to ribbons before he'll yield. Even the young lady cats have this inestimable superiority over human beings that they can fight among themselves, and work off the jealousy, hatred and malice of their lives in a sprawling, yelling combat on a flat roof. All cats fight, and all keep themselves more or less in training while they are young. Your cat may be the acknowledged lightweight champion of his district — a Griffo of the feline ring! Just think how much more he gets out of his life than you do out of yours — what a hurricane of fighting and love-making his life is — and blush for yourself! You have had one little love affair and never a good, all-out fight in your life!

And the sport they have, too! As they get older and retire from the ring they go in for sport more systematically, and the suburban backyards that are to us but dullness indescribable, are to them hunting grounds and trysting places where they may have more sport and adventure than ever had King Arthur's knights or Robin Hood's merry men. Grimalkin decides to go and kill a canary in a neighbouring verandah. Consider the fascination of it — the stealthy reconnaissance from the top of the fence; the care to avoid waking the house dog; the noiseless approach and the hurried dash upon the verandah, and the fierce clawing at the fluttering bird till the mangled body is dragged through the bars of the cage; the exultant retreat with the spoil and the growling over the feast that follows. Not the least entertaining part of it is the demure satisfaction of arriving home in time for breakfast and hearing the house-mistress say, "Tom must be sick; he seems to have no appetite."

It is always levelled as a reproach against cats that they are more fond of their home than of the people in it. Naturally, the cat doesn't like to leave his country, the land where he has got all his friends, and where he knows every landmark. Exiled in a strange land, he would have to learn a new geography, would have to find out all about another tribe of dogs, would have to fight and make love to an entirely new nation of cats. Life isn't long enough for that sort of thing and so, when the family moves, the cat, if allowed, will stay at the old house and attach himself to the new occupiers. He will give them the privilege of boarding him while he enjoys life in his own way. He is not going to sacrifice his whole career for the doubtful reward which fidelity to his old master or mistress might bring.

And if people know so little about cats, how much less do they know about the dog? This article was started as an essay on the dog, and the cat was only incidentally to be referred to, but there was so much to say about cats that they have used up all the space, and a fresh start must be made to deal with the dog — the friend of man.

The Dog

THE CAT is the *roué*, sportsman, gambler, gay Lothario of the animal kingdom. The dog is the workman, a member of society who likes to have his day's work, and does it more conscientiously than most human beings. A dog always looks as if he ought to have a pipe in his mouth and a black bag for his lunch, and then he would go quite happily to the office every day.

A dog without work is like a man without work, a nuisance to himself and everybody else. People who live about town, and keep a dog to give the children hydatids and to keep the neighbours awake at night, imagine that the animal is fulfilling his destiny and is not capable of anything better. All town dogs, fancy dogs, show dogs, lap-dogs, and dogs with no work to do should be at once abolished; it is only in the country that a dog has any justification for his existence.

The old theory that animals have only instinct and not reason is knocked endways by the dog. A dog can reason as well as a human being on some subjects, and better on others; and undoubtedly the best reasoning dog of all is the sheepdog. The sheepdog is a professional artist with a pride in his business. Watch any drover's dogs bringing sheep into the yards. How thoroughly they feel their responsibility, and how very annoyed they get if any stray vagrant dog with no occupation wants them to stop and fool about! They snap at him and hurry off as much as to say, "You go about your idleness. Don't you see this is my busy day?"

Dogs are followers of Carlyle. They hold that the only happiness for a dog in this life is to find his work and to do it. The idle, *dilettante*, non-working aristocratic dog they have no use for.

The training of a sheepdog for his profession begins at a very early age. The first thing is to take him out with his mother and let him see her working. He blunders out lightheartedly, frisking about in front of the horse, and he gets his first lesson that day, for his owner tries to ride over him, and generally succeeds. That teaches him one thing — to keep behind the horse till he is wanted. It is amusing to see how it knocks all the gas out of a puppy, and with what a humble air he falls to the rear and glues himself to the horse's heels, scarcely daring to look to the right or to the left for fear he may commit some other breach of etiquette. Then he watches the old slut work, and is allowed to go with her round the sheep, and, as likely as not, if he shows any disposition to get out of hand and frolic about, the old lady will bite him sharply to prevent his interfering with her work.

Then by degrees, slowly, like any other professional, he learns his business. He learns to bring sheep after a horse simply at a wave of the hand; to force the mob up to a gate where they can be counted or drafted; learns to follow the scent of lost sheep and to drive sheep through a town without any master, one dog going on ahead to block the sheep from turning off into by-streets, while the other drives them on from the rear.

How do they learn all these things? Dogs for show work are taught painstakingly by men who are skilled in handling them, but after all they teach themselves more than the men teach them. There is no doubt that the acquired knowledge of generations is transmitted from dog to dog. The puppy, descended from a race of good sheepdogs, starts with all his faculties directed towards the working of sheep; he is half-educated as soon as he is born. He can no more help working sheep than a born musician can help playing the fiddle, or a Hebrew can help making money. It is bred in him. If he can't get sheep to work, he will work a fowl; and often and often one can see a collie pup painstakingly and carefully driving a bewildered old hen into a stable or a stockyard, or any other enclosed space on which he has fixed his mind. How does he learn to do that? He didn't learn it at all. The knowledge was born with him.

The Dog

It would be interesting to get examples of this inherited ability, and only that I don't want to let a flood of dog-liars loose on the paper, I would suggest to the editor to invite correspondence from those who have seen unquestionable examples of young, untaught animals doing things which they could only have learnt by inheritance.

When the dog has been educated, or educated himself, he enjoys his work; but sometimes, if he thinks he has had enough of it, he will deliberately quit and go home. Very few dogs like work "in the yards". The sun is hot, the dust rises in clouds, and there is nothing to do but bark, bark, bark, which is all very well for learners and amateurs but is beneath the dignity of the true professional sheepdog. Then, when the dogs are hoarse with barking and nearly choked with dust, the men lose their tempers and swear at them, and throw clods of earth at them, and sing out to them, "Speak up, blast you!" At last the dogs suddenly decide that they have done enough for the day, and, watching their opportunity, they silently steal over the fence, and go and hide in any cool place they can find. After a while the men notice that hardly any dogs are left, and then operations are suspended while a great hunt is made into all outlying pieces of cover, where the dogs are sure to be found lying low and looking as guilty as so many thieves. A clutch at the scruff of the neck, a kick in the ribs, and the dog is hauled out of his hiding place, and accompanies his master to the yard, frolicking about and pretending that he is quite delighted to be going back to work, and only happened to have hid in that bush out of sheer thought-lessness. He is a champion hypocrite, is the dog.

After working another ten minutes, he will be over the fences again; and he won't hide in the same place twice. The second time he will be a lot harder to find than the first time.

Dogs, like horses, have very keen intuition. They know when a man is frightened of them, and they know when the men around them are frightened, though they may not know the cause. In the great Queens-land strike, when the shearers attacked Dagworth shed, some rifle vol-leys were exchanged. The shed was burnt, and the air was full of human electricity, each man giving out waves of fear and excitement. Mark now the effect it had on the dogs. They were not in the fighting; nobody fired at them, and nobody spoke to them; but every dog left his master, left the sheep, and went away about six miles to the homestead. There wasn't a dog about the shed next day, after the fight. They knew there was something out of the common in the way of danger. The noise of the rifles would not frighten them, because many of them were dogs that were very fond of going out turkey shooting.

The same thing happened constantly with horses in the South African war. A loose horse would feed contentedly about while his own troops were firing; but when the troops were being fired at, and a bullet or two whistled past, the horses at once became uneasy, and the loose ones would trot away. The noise of a bullet passing cannot have been as terrifying to them as the sound of a rifle going off, but the nervousness and excitement of the men communicated itself to them. There are more capacities in horses and dogs, Horatio, than are dreamt of in your philosophy.

Dogs have an amazing sense of responsibility. Sometimes, when there are sheep to be worked, an old slut, who has young puppies, may be seen greatly exercised in her mind whether she should go out or not. On the one hand, she does not care about leaving the puppies; on the other, she feels that she really ought to go out, and not let the sheep be knocked about by those learners. Hesitatingly, with many a look behind her, she trots out after the horses and the other dogs. An impassioned appeal from the head boundary rider, "Go on back home, will yer!" is treated with the contempt it deserves. She goes out to the yards, works, perhaps half the day, and then slips quietly under the fences and trots off home contented.

Besides the sheepdog there are hunting, sporting, and fighting dogs who all devote themselves to their professions with a diligence that might well be copied by human beings; there is no animal so thoroughly in earnest as a dog. But this article is now long enough. Hunting, sporting and fighting dogs must be dealt with at another time; and, meanwhile, any readers who can forward any striking instances of canine sagacity should write same out in ink on one side of the paper only, get them attested by a missionary, mark them "Dog Story", and forward them to this office, where they will, as a rule, be carefully burnt.

The Old Timer's Steeplechase

The sheep were shorn and the wool went down
    At the time of our local racing:
And I'd earned a spell — I was burnt and brown —
So I rolled my swag for a trip to town
    And a look at the steeplechasing.

'Twas rough and ready — an uncleared course
    As rough as the blacks had found it;
With barbed wire fences, topped with gorse,
And a water jump that would drown a horse,
    And the steeple three times round it.

There was never a fence the tracks to guard —
    Some straggling posts defined 'em:
And the day was hot, and the drinking hard,
Till none of the stewards could see a yard
    Before nor yet behind 'em!

But the bell was rung and the nags were out,
    Excepting an old outsider
Whose trainer started an awful rout,
For his boy had gone on a drinking bout
    And left him without a rider.

"Is there not one man in the crowd," he cried,
    "In the whole of the crowd so clever,
Is there not one man that will take a ride
On the old white horse from the northern side
    That was bred on the Mooki River?"

'Twas an old white horse that they called The Cow,
    And a cow would look well beside him;
But I was pluckier then than now
(And I wanted excitement anyhow),
    So at last I agreed to ride him.

And the trainer said, ''Well, he's dreadful slow,
    And he hasn't a chance whatever;
But I'm stony broke, so it's time to show
A trick or two that the trainers know
    Who train by the Mooki River.

''The first time round at the further side,
    With the trees and the scrub about you,
Just pull behind them and run out wide
And then dodge into the scrub and hide,
    And let them go round without you.

''At the third time round, for the final spin
    With the pace, and the dust to blind 'em,
They'll never notice if you chip in
For the last half-mile — you'll be sure to win,
    And they'll think you raced behind 'em.

''At the water jump you may have to swim —
    He hasn't a hope to clear it —
Unless he skims like the swallows skim
At full speed over, but not for him!
    He'll never go next or near it.

''But don't you worry — just plunge across,
    For he swims like a well-trained setter.
Then hide away in the scrub and gorse
The rest will be far ahead of course —
    The further ahead the better.

''You must rush the jumps in the last half-round
    For fear that he might refuse 'em;
He'll try to baulk with you, I'll be bound,
Take whip and spurs on the mean old hound,
    And don't be afraid to use 'em.

''At the final round, when the field are slow
    And you are quite fresh to meet 'em,
Sit down, and hustle him all you know
With the whip and spurs, and he'll have to go —
    Remember, you've *got* to beat 'em!''

The flag went down and we seemed to fly,
    And we made the timbers shiver
Of the first big fence, as the stand flashed by,
And I caught the ring of the trainer's cry:
    ''Go on! For the Mooki River!''

73

I jammed him in with a well-packed crush,
   And recklessly — out for slaughter —
Like a living wave over fence and brush
We swept and swung with a flying rush,
   Till we came to the dreaded water.

Ha, ha! I laugh at it now to think
   Of the way I contrived to work it.
Shut in amongst them, before you'd wink,
He found himself on the water's brink,
   With never a chance to shirk it!

The thought of the horror he felt beguiles
   The heart of this grizzled rover!
He gave a snort you could hear for miles,
And a spring would have cleared the Channel Isles
   And carried me safely over!

Then we neared the scrub, and I pulled him back
   In the shade where the gum leaves quiver:
And I waited there in the shadows black
While the rest of the horses, round the track,
   Went on like a rushing river!

At the second round, as the field swept by,
   I saw that the pace was telling;
But on they thundered, and by and by
As they passed the stand I could hear the cry
   Of the folk in the distance, yelling!

Then the last time round! And the hoofbeats rang!
   And I said, "Well, it's now or never!"
And out on the heels of the throng I sprang,
And the spurs bit deep and the whipcord sang
   As I rode! For the Mooki River!

We raced for home in a cloud of dust
   And the curses rose in chorus.
'Twas flog, and hustle, and jump you must!
And The Cow ran well — but to my disgust
   There was one got home before us.

'Twas a big black horse, that I had not seen
   In the part of the race I'd ridden;
And his coat was cool and his rider clean,
And I thought that perhaps I had not been
   The only one that had hidden.

And the trainer came with a visage blue
    With rage, when the race concluded:
Said he, ''I thought you'd have pulled us through,
But the man on the black horse planted too,
    And nearer to home than you did!''

Alas to think that those times so gay
    Have vanished and passed forever!
You don't believe in the yarn you say?
Why, man! 'Twas a matter of every day
    When we raced on the Mooki River!

A Bushman's Song

I'm travellin' down the Castlereagh, and I'm a station hand,
   I'm handy with the ropin' pole, I'm handy with the brand,
And I can ride a rowdy colt, or swing the axe all day,
But there's no demand for a station hand along the Castlereagh.

So it's shift, boys, shift, for there isn't the slightest doubt
That we've got to make a shift to the stations further out
With the packhorse runnin' after, for he follows like a dog,
We must strike across the country at the old jig-jog.

This old black horse I'm riding — if you'll notice what's his brand,
He wears the crooked R, you see — none better in the land.
He takes a lot of beatin', and the other day we tried,
For a bit of a joke, with a racing bloke, for twenty pounds aside.

It was shift, boys, shift, for there wasn't the slightest doubt,
That I had to make him shift, for the money was nearly out;
But he cantered home a winner, with the other one at the flog —
He's a red-hot sort to pick up with his old jig-jog.

I went to Illawarra where my brother's got a farm,
He has to ask his landlord's leave before he lifts his arm;
The landlord owns the countryside — man, woman, dog, and cat,
They haven't the cheek to dare to speak without they touch their hat.

It was shift, boys, shift, for there wasn't the slightest doubt
Their little landlord god and I would soon have fallen out;
Was I to touch my hat to him? — was I his bloomin' dog?
So I makes for up the country at the old jig-jog.

But it's time that I was movin', I've a mighty way to go
Till I drink artesian water from a thousand feet below;
Till I meet the overlanders with the cattle comin' down,
And I'll work a while till I make a pile, then have a spree in town.

So, it's shift, boys, shift, for there isn't the slightest doubt
We've got to make a shift to the stations further out;
The packhorse runs behind us, for he follows like a dog,
And we cross a lot of country at the old jig-jog.

The Man from Goondiwindi, Q.

I

This is the sunburnt bushman who
  Came down from Goondiwindi, Q.

II

This is the Push from Waterloo
That spotted the sunburnt bushman who
Came down from Goondiwindi, Q.

III

These are the wealthy uncles — two,
Part of the Push from Waterloo
That spotted the sunburnt bushman who
Came down from Goondiwindi, Q.

IV

This is the game, by no means new,
Played by the wealthy uncles — two,
Part of the Push from Waterloo
That spotted the sunburnt bushman who
Came down from Goondiwindi, Q.

V

This is the trooper dressed in blue
Who busted the game by no means new
Played by the wealthy uncles — two,
Part of the Push from Waterloo
That spotted the sunburnt bushman who
Came down from Goondiwindi, Q.

VI

This is the magistrate who knew
Not only the trooper dressed in blue,
But also the game by no means new,
And likewise the wealthy uncles — two,
And ditto the Push from Waterloo
That spotted the sunburnt bushman who
Came down from Goondiwindi, Q.

VII

This is the tale that has oft gone through
On western plains where the skies are blue,
Till the native bear and the kangaroo
Have heard of the magistrate who knew
Not only the trooper dressed in blue,
But also the game by no means new,
And likewise the wealthy uncles — two,
And ditto the Push from Waterloo
That spotted the sunburnt bushman who
Came down from Goondiwindi, Q.

Weary Will

The strongest creature for his size
    But least equipped for combat
That dwells beneath Australian skies
    Is Weary Will the Wombat.

He digs his homestead underground,
    He's neither shrewd nor clever;
For kangaroos can leap and bound
    But wombats dig for ever.

The boundary rider's netting fence
    Excites his irritation;
It is to his untutored sense
    His pet abomination.

And when to pass it he desires,
    Upon his task he'll centre
And dig a hole beneath the wires
    Through which the dingoes enter.

And when to block the hole they strain
    With logs and stones and rubble,
Bill Wombat digs it out again
    Without the slightest trouble.

The boundary rider bows to fate,
    Admits he's made a blunder,
And rigs a little swinging gate
    To let Bill Wombat under.

So most contentedly he goes
    Between his haunt and burrow:
He does the only thing he knows,
    And does it very thorough.

Weary Will

The boundary rider's netting fence
Excites his irritation page 80

The Man from Ironbark

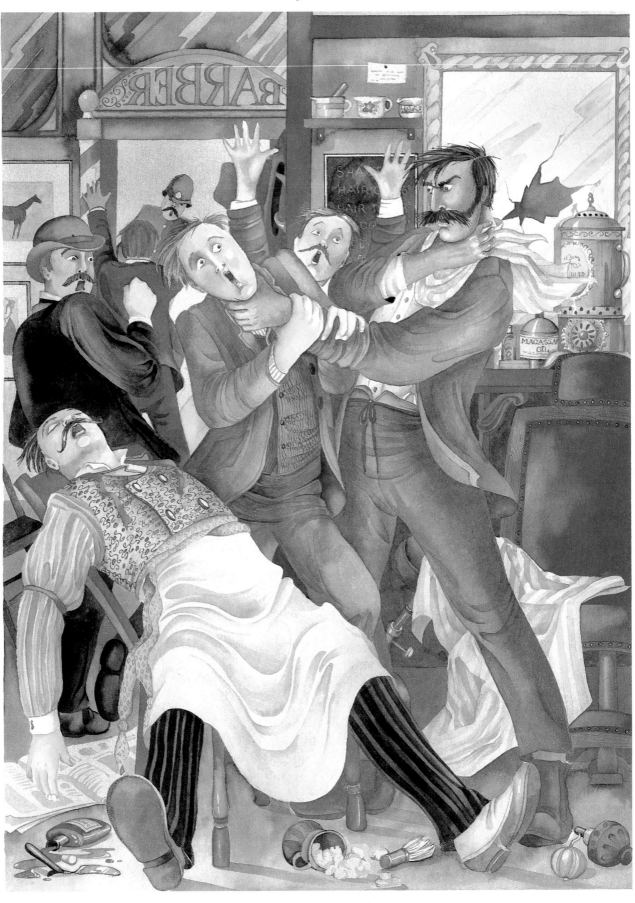

He grabbed the nearest gilded youth, and tried to break his neck.   page 82

The Man from Ironbark

It was the man from Ironbark who struck the Sydney town,
    He wandered over street and park, he wandered up and down.
He loitered here, he loitered there, till he was like to drop,
Until at last in sheer despair he sought a barber's shop.
'''Ere! shave my beard and whiskers off, I'll be a man of mark,
I'll go and do the Sydney toff up home in Ironbark.''

The barber man was small and flash, as barbers mostly are,
He wore a strike-your-fancy sash, he smoked a huge cigar;
He was a humorist of note and keen at repartee,
He laid the odds and kept a ''tote'', whatever that may be,
And when he saw our friend arrive, he whispered, ''Here's a lark!
Just watch me catch him all alive, this man from Ironbark.''

There were some gilded youths that sat along the barber's wall.
Their eyes were dull, their heads were flat, they had no brains at all;
To them the barber passed the wink, his dexter eyelid shut,
''I'll make this bloomin' yokel think his bloomin' throat is cut.''
And as he soaped and rubbed it in he made a rude remark:
''I s'pose the flats is pretty green up there in Ironbark.''

A grunt was all reply he got; he shaved the bushman's chin,
Then made the water boiling hot and dipped the razor in.
He raised his hand, his brow grew black, he paused awhile to gloat,
Then slashed the red-hot razor-back across his victim's throat;
Upon the newly-shaven skin it made a livid mark —
No doubt it fairly took him in — the man from Ironbark.

He fetched a wild up-country yell might wake the dead to hear,
And though his throat, he knew full well, was cut from ear to ear,
He struggled gamely to his feet, and faced the murd'rous foe:
''You've done for me! you dog, I'm beat! one hit before I go!
I only wish I had a knife, you blessed murdering shark!
But you'll remember all your life the man from Ironbark.''

He lifted up his hairy paw, with one tremendous clout
He landed on the barber's jaw, and knocked the barber out.
He set to work with nail and tooth, he made the place a wreck;
He grabbed the nearest gilded youth, and tried to break his neck.
And all the while his throat he held to save his vital spark,
And "Murder! Bloody murder!" yelled the man from Ironbark.

A peeler man who heard the din came in to see the show;
He tried to run the bushman in, but he refused to go.
And when at last the barber spoke, and said "'Twas all in fun —
'Twas just a little harmless joke, a trifle overdone."
"A joke!" he cried, "By George, that's fine; a lively sort of lark;
I'd like to catch that murdering swine some night in Ironbark."

And now while round the shearing floor the list'ning shearers gape,
He tells the story o'er and o'er, and brags of his escape.
"Them barber chaps what keeps a tote, By George, I've had enough,
One tried to cut my bloomin' throat, but thank the Lord it's tough."
And whether he's believed or no, there's one thing to remark,
That flowing beards are all the go way up in Ironbark.

Constantine the Great

ARRIVAL at "LIMESTONE"

THE THOROUGHBRED MARES in their own exclusive paddock at Limestone stud were a very aristocratic lot, and as keen on their own dignity and precedence as a lot of patrician dowagers in a Court drawing-room: consequently, they were very much upset when a strange horse was turned in among them one bright December morning, without their permission being asked or their desires considered in any way whatever.

You must understand that these highly pedigreed ladies all figured in the pages of the *Stud Book*, which is the *Debrett's Peerage* of the Turf world, and they knew each other's pedigrees and relationships away back into the days of Charles I. Not a horse could win an important race in any part of the world and no mare could produce a Derby winner, but what such of the Limestone ladies as were related to the new celebrity became very proud and arrogant, and those who were not related became jealous — very jealous indeed.

Being a lot of highly bred dowagers, they were divided into as many cliques and coteries as the countesses and duchesses in a Mayfair drawing-room, and the credentials of any new arrival were very closely scanned before she was admitted to any of the more exclusive circles.

"That mare," a dowager countess would say, on considering the pedigree of a new arrival, "of course I shall call on her, but I really couldn't make a friend of her. My dear, do you know that her family haven't won a really big race for three generations?"

Besides an infinite number of smaller coteries, there were two clear-cut social sets among the mares — those born in England, and those born in Australia.

The English mares did not actually patronise the others, but they just tolerated them, and on Derby Day the English mares got together and talked about Epsom and Newmarket till the other mares could hardly bear it: and a pert young Australian mare, after listening to as much of this conversation as she could stand, said, "The Epsom Derby! That's the race where they go up and down hills, isn't it, like our stockhorses go after cattle?" a remark that was passed over in a kind of pitying silence. But in spite of their bickering among themselves they presented a united front against all outsiders, and they looked upon any horse not in the *Stud Book* in much the same way as a duchess would look upon the bride of a costermonger.

And so, on this beautiful December day, a strange horse was actually being turned into their paddock, a big gaunt bay horse with hair on his fetlocks, a plain head and spur marks on his ribs: a horse that looked as though he ought to be carrying a general at the head of an army, so strong and resolute was his appearance, and so kind and intelligent was his eye; but the hair on his fetlocks, the spur marks on his ribs, and the plainness of his head decided the mares that he could not be a thoroughbred — perhaps something very near it, but not quite born in the purple. So they decided to ignore the intruder, and they cast calm supercilious glances at him as he strolled past them on his way to the river to get a drink.

The two men who had brought him to the paddock stood chatting by the rails. The mares knew one of them well enough, for the tall man with the heavy moustache and the slow soft way of speaking was Gordon Macallister, owner of the Limestone stud, and he was a personal friend of every mare in the paddock. He visited them nearly every day, he looked after them when they were sick and a word from him in praise of one of the foals was enough to make that foal's mother proud and joyful for a week.

The keen-eyed little man with the quick, staccato way of speaking was unknown to the mares and they put him down as not much class anyway; if they had known that he was Ike Heronshaw, the greatest trainer of the day, they would have been more impressed.

"Well, Ike," said Macallister, "this is the best I can do for you. No one goes through this paddock, and no one would dream of looking for him among my crack mares and foals. Why does his owner want him planted?"

"He's broke."

"Broke! I thought he had plenty of money."

"So he did have. But he wanted more, so he bought half the wool in Australia and shipped it and struck a misere hand. He's got no ready money, y'understand, and his creditors are after him, and if they can get hold of this horse they'll sell him by order of the Court. But the market's risin' and if he can hold on for a few weeks he'll be all right again. That's why he wants this horse out of the road."

"I see. But I'm taking a risk putting him in with my mares and foals. I wouldn't dream of doing it for anybody but you. Is he quiet?"

"Quiet! You could bowl hedgehogs at his hind legs all day and he wouldn't kick at 'em. Your daughter could ride him, so then nobody would tumble to it that he is anything more than an ordinary hack. What I'm afraid of is that he might cripple himself if he gets galloping about with these foals."

"That's what you're afraid of, is it? Well, what about me, taking the risk of turning a stranger into this paddock? He might set the whole lot racing for their lives! If I'll chance my mares and foals, you've got to chance your horse. If I put him anywhere else, somebody's sure to see him and you'll have the bailiffs after him."

With that, the two men rode away to the homestead and the mares were left to size up the intruder.

Possibly the most aristocratic mare in the paddock was Lady Susan, a descendant of the great St Simon, and with so many other celebrated relatives that her position was almost unchallengeable. True, she was Australian-born, but her grandsire had won the English Derby and she herself had won the Australian Oaks, and what was more important, her foals had won two Derbies and a Melbourne Cup. The English mares might affect to despise Australian races, but any foal from Lady Susan was worth five thousand guineas as it stood on its delicate little hoofs alongside her in the paddock. The English mares might talk about Epsom and Newmarket, but none of their foals averaged five thousand guineas, so there was no more to be said: all the mares waited for a lead from Lady Susan in most matters, but in regard to this new horse they thought they were on safe ground in criticising him.

The chorus was led off by Cat's Cradle, a young and pert Australian mare who was inclined to give herself airs because her full sister had won the last big race for two-year-old fillies by three lengths in very fast time. She was addicted to slang and after looking the newcomer over in a very supercilious way she gave a horse laugh, which is a kind of internal laugh that you can't see.

"Girls," she said, "what have we here? Pipe the marks of the harpoons on his ribs, and the whiskers on his fetlocks! I'll bet he's a winner — the winner of the Big Scrub Handicap with the first prize a bees' nest. After you've won the race, they show you the bees' nest in a tree, and you have to cut the tree down and rob the nest for yourself."

Meanwhile the English mares were muttering among themselves such remarks as "preposterous", "wouldn't be tolerated in England", "you never know what to expect in this extraordinary country", being faintly heard above the singing of Featherbrain, an English mare who was apt to be a bit hysterical, who screamed to her foal and set off up the paddock as hard as she could split, but finding that none of the others followed her, returned in a shamefaced way to the mob. All this time old Lady Susan had said nothing until her foal, who was quite an important person, for he was expected to fetch at least six thousand guineas at auction, went up to her and said, "Mother, can I go and speak to the new horse? He seems so lonely, and none of the others will go near him."

"Yes," she said, "you can go. I seem to see a likeness in that horse to somebody I used to know. I think I must have raced against his mother at some time or other. You mustn't say anything rude to him about the hair on his fetlocks, for sometimes that comes to us from the old English horses that were in the pedigrees hundreds of years before the Arabs were ever brought into England. Just be civil to him, and if he tells you anything come back and tell me,'' — for even the greatest ladies are not above a little curiosity.

Without the slightest hesitation, Lady Susan's foal marched up to the newcomer and gave him the usual Australian salutation, ''Good day. It looks very dry, doesn't it?''

The stranger, who appeared to be a rough and ready sort of person, said, ''Yes, it's dry all right: and who may you be, young fellow?''

To which the foal, who had a great idea of his own importance though he was only a few months old, answered without any trepidation, ''I'm Lady Susan's foal. Perhaps you've heard of my full brother Gaslight?''

''Gaslight!'' said the stranger. ''Why I ran against'' — and here he stopped as though about to say too much. ''I ran against a stone coming up, and bruised my heel a bit. But look here, young fellow, it doesn't matter what you are full brother to. The thing is, can you gallop yourself? The Judge don't place any horse first because he's full brother to something, you know.''

''Oh, yes, I know that. But I can go a bit, and when the foals all get together for our gallop round the paddock this evening, you can see me travel. Did you ever do any racing yourself?''

''Oh yes, young fellow, I've raced a bit: not as much as some and more than others. The less you talk about what you can do in racing the better for you, you understand. The handicapper might hear you, and you'd never get the weight off. But I'll watch you go round this evening, and I might be able to give you a wrinkle or two that will do you some good when your time comes to go to the barrier.''

That evening when the foals gathered for their customary sprint round the paddock, the stranger watched them for a while and then tossed up his head and set after them, going in surprising fashion, his great strides eating up the ground, while the foals with their little nostrils distended and their little hoofs rattling on the stony ridges strove valiantly for the lead. The Featherbrain mare got very excited and said, ''Look, look, he'll kill the foals'', to which Lady Susan, who had picked up some hard sayings in the training stables, replied, ''Shut your head! The foals are all right.''

You see, her foal was well in front and going like a champion.

After the gallop Lady Susan's foal strolled over to the stranger expecting to get all sorts of compliments, but the stranger was not of the gushing type. ''Very fair,'' he said. ''Very fair, but look here, youngster, when you first jump off, don't make too big a jump. It's all right with nothing on your back, but when you've got a jockey there, too big a jump will unbalance him. Just take half a stride as you move out of the barrier, and get the weight on your back under way. Then get down to it and deal it out to 'em all you know. Give my compliments to your mother and tell her I know all about her. Everybody on the Turf knows all about Lady Susan.''

THE FIRE

That was the year of the big bushfire, the fire that swept up the river from a hundred miles south, burning all before it. It had been a great season, and the long grass and thistles on the flats were as dry as tinder, and the wind brought the fire along in great leaps, the burning cinders being carried by the wind from the dry trees to start fresh fires half a mile ahead. When the breeze brought the first scent of the burning gum leaves, and the clouds of smoke appeared over the distant hills, the mares gathered themselves and their foals together sniffing with pointed ears at the new terror — something of which none of them had had any experience whatever.

It so happened that Macallister was away from the head station that day, and he only arrived in his car as night fell, bringing with him his daughter, Jean, a fourteen-year-old girl with just as much interest in the horses as Macallister himself. She had been riding ever since she could remember anything, ever since the days when she was carried as a baby in front of her father's saddle.

Springing from the car, Macallister dragged a bridle out of the tonneau, and walking in a quiet matter-of-fact way he went up to the stranger and slipped the bridle on him, talking to him in a soothing voice all the time. Then he led him up to the car and told his daughter what she must do.

"Jean," he said, "that fire will be here in ten minutes and all I've got in the world is in these mares and foals. There's only one thing that can save them, and that is this horse. This is Constantine the Great, the horse that won both the Sydney and Melbourne Derbies and the Melbourne Cup. You'll have to ride him bareback, for there's no time to go and get a saddle, but they say he's very quiet. Now listen to what I've got to tell you.

"As soon as I let the mares and foals out of this paddock, they'll go like mad things all over the bush, and half of them will be crippled or killed in the darkness: but if you can keep ahead of them for the first mile, they'll follow you and you can lead them up to the big bald hill where there's no grass and no timber. When you get them there, try and keep them there — do your best anyhow. They'll be pretty tired by that time and if you keep on riding round and round, and calling out to them in the darkness they may follow you and it may save the lot.

"And now there's another thing. There's that gate at the Two Mile. You'll have no time to stop and open it or the mares will scatter all over the place. Run him right slap into it, and send it flying. It opens in the middle and his weight will smash it like paper. Don't stop for anything and don't look behind you. The mares will follow you through the gate and the main thing is to keep ahead of them the first mile. If there's a horse in the world that can keep ahead of those thoroughbred mares with nothing on their backs, this is the one. I did not want him here, but it looks as if he might save us.

"As soon as I get you away, I'll go up to the house and tell your mother to hide in the river if the fire comes, and then I'll go back to try and save that old crippled woman down in the hut on the flat."

Even as he spoke a red glare showed down at the bend of the river and the mares grew terrified. Swinging the girl on to the big horse's back, he led him towards the gate, patting him on the neck, and talking to him.

"Old man," he said, "you're running for a big stake tonight. Bigger than the Melbourne Cup. There's a hundred thousand pounds of money in these mares and there's my little girl's life. It's up to you to save them, so now go to it like a thoroughbred.''

By this time they had reached the gate, the big horse walking quite unconcerned, while the terrified mares crowded behind him.

Giving his daughter a hurried kiss, Macallister threw the gate open, and with the big horse in front, the wild cavalcade swept away into the darkness.

For the first half mile Jean knew nothing but the great swinging strides of the horse beneath her, the dimly seen stretch of track in front, and behind her the roaring of hundreds of hoofs, and the mares whinnying and calling to their foals. If she came off, or if the big horse made a false step in the darkness and came down, she would be trodden flat in an instant by the terrified rush of the mares behind her: but there was a wild exhilaration in the ride that banished all thought of fear. Constantine the Great lay down to work without fear or excitement, for it was nothing new to him to hear the drumming of a field of horses behind him. Some instinct inherited from his Arab ancestors made him reach out and clear in his stride the little waterways that crossed the track. Once or twice in the headlong flight the girl's knee grazed perilously against the trees, and more than once she had to lie flat down on his neck to avoid being swept off by an overhanging branch: but still the great machine-like stride swept him along in front of the mares, and still they followed in close formation at his heels. After a while the pace slackened and Jean was able to sit up and call out to the mares, who knew her voice and answered her with shrill neighs: but the pace was still fast enough to make any delay risky and Jean knew that if she stopped to open the Two Mile gate the mares would probably swing on down the fence into the darkness and smash themselves up in the scrub.

Having got so far in safety, her spirits rose and she amused herself by talking to the big horse as they swept along.

''There's a gate ahead of us,'' she said, ''and you've got to smash it or these mares and foals will be killed. Will you do it for me? Don't jump it, or I'll very likely come off, for I'm not very good at jumping fences barebacked, and if the mares follow you over it, that will be the end of me.''

Luckily, the gate was hidden under the shadow of some trees, and the big horse was on it before he saw it.

With no time to jump he gave a snort of defiance and raced straight into it.

Smash! The two by four hardwood battens were splintered like matches under the weight of the blow, and without pause or hesitation he swept on while the mares crowded and crushed through the gap that he had left. So instantaneous had been the smash that Jean had hardly been shifted on her precarious perch, but with each stride that the big horse took she felt something moist on her hands. She was puzzled to think what it could be, but at last she realised that the horse had cut himself rather badly on the gate and that his blood was splashing up on to her hands and clothes. For the first time in that wild ride she felt utterly miserable, but there was nothing that could be done about it so she held her course through the rough timber for the Bald Hill.

Arriving at the hill, she found that an advanced wing of the fire had nearly cut her off, and everything was red flames, smoke, and confusion. In a sort of sanctuary on top of the hill, all sorts of bush animals had gathered, wallabies and kangaroos bewildered with terror racing madly round and round, while rabbits with their fur on fire rushed screaming across the open. A mob of emus, all fear of mankind forgotten, trotted up to her and almost stuck their heads in her face as though asking for guidance. Coming up at their ungainly trot, they had cut the mob of mares in two, and for a moment it looked as though one wing of the mares would lose their heads and race into the scrub; but just as things hung in the balance a foal trotted towards her from the outlying mob, his mother followed him, and in another moment all the mares had gathered together again.

By the light of the burning trees Jean recognised the foal that had so unexpectedly come to her help at a critical moment. "Why," she said, "it's Silas! And he seems to know this horse! Aren't you frightened, Silas?" But Silas, with his small nostrils sniffing the smoke, was quite at his ease, and appeared to think that Providence would hesitate before destroying a gentleman of his quality.

Ringed with smoke and fire, and hampered by terrified wild animals, Jean rode backwards and forwards through the night, keeping the mares together and vainly trying to see what injury her mount had sustained. She dared not get off the horse lest she should never be able to get on again, but as daylight broke she was able to see a big raw gash across his chest from which the blood still welled and, overcome with weariness and excitement, she burst into tears.

A few hours later a big gaunt horse with bloodstained chest and forelegs, and ridden by an inexpressibly weary little girl, led the Limestone mares back to the homestead. Here she found the lucerne paddocks had saved the house from destruction, and after receiving the frantically excited greetings of her father and mother, her first thought was of the injury that her horse had sustained at the gate. After examination her father pronounced it only superficial, and it was a thankful girl that tumbled into bed to sleep off the recollections of the night amidst the fire.

When things had settled down a bit in the horse paddock once more, Lady Susan marched up to the stranger and said, "We have to thank you for saving our lives. Do you mind telling me your name? These English ladies and myself are now of the opinion that you must be a far more important person than you look."

"Well ma'am," he said, "I have a name all right. Such as it is you may have heard it, for they call me Constantine the Great. As for importance, well, I've won some races and I've lost others. I've raced against some of your foals and you want to look after that little fellow you have now, for a gamer bit of stuff I never saw.''

When the mares discovered who he was, there was great excitement in hunting over his pedigree, and it was found that he was first cousin to fifteen of them, and was more or less distantly related to every mare in the paddock. It took them several days to hunt out all the relationships.

A few months later the leading newspaper starred the item: ''Constantine the Great has come back to work, and appears to be in great fettle except that his chest is disfigured by a scar which he no doubt sustained while playing about in the paddock. It does not give him any trouble and he is certain to add to his already imposing record of wins.''

Saltbush Bill's Second Fight

The news came down on the Castlereagh, and went to the world at
   large,
That twenty thousand travelling sheep, with Saltbush Bill in charge,
Were drifting down from a dried-out run to ravage the Castlereagh;
And the squatters swore when they heard the news, and wished they
   were well away:
For the name and the fame of Saltbush Bill were over the countryside
For the wonderful way that he fed his sheep, and the dodges and tricks
   he tried.
He would lose his way on a Main Stock Route, and stray to the
   squatters' grass;
He would come to a run with the boss away, and swear he had leave
   to pass;
And back of all and behind it all, as well the squatters knew,
If he had to fight, he would fight all day, so long as his sheep got
   through:
But this is the story of Stingy Smith, the owner of Hard Times Hill,
And the way that he chanced on a fighting man to reckon with Saltbush
   Bill.

'Twas Stingy Smith on his stockyard sat, and prayed for an early spring,
When he stared at sight of a clean-shaved tramp, who walked with
   jaunty swing;
For a clean-shaved tramp with a jaunty walk a-swinging along the track
Is as rare a thing as a feathered frog on the desolate roads outback.
So the tramp he made for the travellers' hut, and asked could he camp
   the night;
But Stingy Smith had a bright idea, and he said to him, "Can you
   fight?"
"Why, what's the game?" said the clean-shaved tramp, as he looked at
   him up and down —
"If you want a battle, get off that fence, and I'll kill you for half-a-
   crown!

But, Boss, you'd better not fight with me, it wouldn't be fair nor right;
I'm Stiffener Joe, from the Rocks Brigade, and I killed a man in a fight:
I served two years for it, fair and square, and now I'm a trampin' back,
To look for a peaceful quiet life away on the outside track —"
"Oh, it's not myself, but a drover chap," said Stingy Smith with glee;
"A bullying fellow, called Saltbush Bill — and you are the man for me.
He's on the road with his hungry sheep, and he's certain to raise a row,
For he's bullied the whole of the Castlereagh till he's got them under
    cow —
Just pick a quarrel and raise a fight, and leather him good and hard,
And I'll take good care that his wretched sheep don't wander a half a
    yard.
It's a five-pound job if you belt him well — do anything short of kill,
For there isn't a beak on the Castlereagh will fine you for Saltbush
    Bill."

"I'll take the job," said the fighting man, "and hot as this cove appears,
He'll stand no chance with a bloke like me, what's lived on the game
    for years;
For he's maybe learnt in a boxing school, and sparred for a round or so,
But I've fought all hands in a ten foot ring each night in a travelling
    show;
They earnt a pound if they stayed three rounds, and they tried for it
    every night —
In a ten foot ring! Oh, that's the game that teaches a bloke to fight,
For they'd rush and clinch, it was Dublin Rules, and we drew no colour
    line;
And they all tried hard for to earn the pound, but they got no pound of
    mine:
If I saw no chance in the opening round I'd slog at their wind, and wait
Till an opening came — and it *always* came — and I settled 'em, sure
    as fate;
Left on the ribs and right on the jaw — and, when the chance comes,
    make sure!
And it's there a professional bloke like me gets home on an amateur:

"For it's my experience every day, and I make no doubt it's yours,
That a third-class pro is an over-match for the best of the amateurs —"
"Oh, take your swag to the travellers' hut," said Smith, "for you waste
    your breath;
You've a first-class chance, if you lose the fight, of talking your man
    to death.
I'll tell the cook you're to have your grub, and see that you eat your fill,
And come to the scratch all fit and well to leather this Saltbush Bill."
'Twas Saltbush Bill, and his travelling sheep were wending their weary
    way

Saltbush Bill's Second Fight

On the Main Stock Route, through the Hard Times Run, on their six-
 mile stage a day;
And he strayed a mile from the Main Stock Route, and started to feed
 along,
And, when Stingy Smith came up, Bill said that the Route was surveyed
 wrong;
And he tried to prove that the sheep had rushed and strayed from their
 camp at night,
But the fighting man he kicked Bill's dog, and of course that meant a
 fight:

So they sparred and fought, and they shifted ground and never a sound
 was heard
But the thudding fists on their brawny ribs, and the seconds' muttered
 word,
Till the fighting man shot home his left on the ribs with a mighty clout,
And his right flashed up with a half-arm blow — and Saltbush Bill
 ''went out''.
He fell face down, and towards the blow; and their hearts with fear were
 filled,
For he lay as still as a fallen tree, and they thought that he must be
 killed.
So Stingy Smith and the fighting man, they lifted him from the ground,
And sent to home for a brandy flask, and they slowly fetched him
 round;
But his head was bad, and his jaw was hurt — in fact, he could scarcely
 speak —
So they let him spell till he got his wits, and he camped on the run a
 week,
While the travelling sheep went here and there, wherever they liked to
 stray,
Till Saltbush Bill was fit once more for the track to the Castlereagh.

Then Stingy Smith he wrote a note, and gave to the fighting man:
'Twas writ to the boss of the neighbouring run, and thus the missive
 ran:
''The man with this is a fighting man, one Stiffener Joe by name;
He came near murdering Saltbush Bill, and I found it a costly game:
But it's worth your while to employ the chap, for there isn't the
 slightest doubt
You'll have no trouble from Saltbush Bill while this man hangs
 about —''
But an answer came by the next week's mail, with news that might
 well appal:
''The man you sent with a note is not a fighting man at all!

He has shaved his beard, and has cut his hair, but I spotted him at a
    look;
He is Tom Devine, who has worked for years for Saltbush Bill as cook.
Bill coached him up in the fighting yarn, and taught him the tale by
    rote,
And they shammed to fight, and they got your grass and divided your
    five-pound note.
'Twas a clean take-in, and you'll find it wise — 'twill save you a lot
    of pelf —
When next you're hiring a fighting man, just fight him a round
    yourself.''

And the teamsters out on the Castlereagh, when they meet with a week
    of rain,
And the waggon sinks to its axle-tree, deep down in the black soil plain,
When the bullocks wade in a sea of mud, and strain at the load of wool,
And the cattle dogs at the bullocks' heels are biting to make them pull,
When the offside driver flays the team, and curses them while he flogs,
And the air is thick with the language used, and the clamour of men
    and dogs —
The teamsters say, as they pause to rest and moisten each hairy throat,
They wish they could swear like Stingy Smith when he read that
    neighbour's note.

Clancy of The Overflow

I had written him a letter which I had, for want of better
    Knowledge, sent to where I met him down the Lachlan, years ago,
He was shearing when I knew him, so I sent the letter to him,
    Just "on spec", addressed as follows: "Clancy, of The Overflow".

And an answer came directed in a writing unexpected,
    (And I think the same was written with a thumbnail dipped in tar)
'Twas his shearing mate who wrote it, and *verbatim* I will quote it:
    "Clancy's gone to Queensland droving, and we don't know where he are."

In my wild erratic fancy visions come to me of Clancy
    Gone a-droving "down the Cooper" where the western drovers go;
As the stock are slowly stringing, Clancy rides behind them singing,
    For the drover's life has pleasures that the townsfolk never know.

And the bush hath friends to meet him, and their kindly voices greet him
    In the murmur of the breezes and the river on its bars,
And he sees the vision splendid of the sunlit plains extended,
    And at night the wondrous glory of the everlasting stars.

I am sitting in my dingy little office, where a stingy
    Ray of sunlight struggles feebly down between the houses tall,
And the foetid air and gritty of the dusty, dirty city
    Through the open window floating, spreads its foulness over all.

And in place of lowing cattle, I can hear the fiendish rattle
    Of the tramways and the buses making hurry down the street,
And the language uninviting of the gutter children fighting,
    Comes fitfully and faintly through the ceaseless tramp of feet.

And the hurrying people daunt me, and their pallid faces haunt me
    As they shoulder one another in their rush and nervous haste,
With their eager eyes and greedy, and their stunted forms and weedy,
    For townsfolk have no time to grow, they have no time to waste.

And I somehow rather fancy that I'd like to change with Clancy,
    Like to take a turn at droving where the seasons come and go,
While he faced the round eternal of the cashbook and the journal —
    But I doubt he'd suit the office, Clancy, of "The Overflow".

Clancy of The Overflow

*In my wild erratic fancy visions come to me of Clancy
Gone a-droving "down the Cooper" where the western drovers go*   page 96

Mulga Bill's Bicycle

*And then as Mulga Bill let out one last despairing shriek
It made a leap of twenty feet into the Dead Man's Creek*   page 97

Mulga Bill's Bicycle

'Twas Mulga Bill, from Eaglehawk, that caught the cycling craze;
He turned away the good old horse that served him many days;
He dressed himself in cycling clothes, resplendent to be seen;
He hurried off to town and bought a shining new machine;
And as he wheeled it through the door, with air of lordly pride,
The grinning shop assistant said, "Excuse me, can you ride?"

"See here, young man," said Mulga Bill, "from Walgett to the sea,
From Conroy's Gap to Castlereagh, there's none can ride like me.
I'm good all round at everything, as everybody knows,
Although I'm not the one to talk — I *hate* a man that blows.
But riding is my special gift, my chiefest, sole delight;
Just ask a wild duck can it swim, a wildcat can it fight.
There's nothing clothed in hair or hide, or built of flesh or steel,
There's nothing walks or jumps, or runs, on axle, hoof, or wheel,
But what I'll sit, while hide will hold and girths and straps are tight:
I'll ride this here two-wheeled concern right straight away at sight."

'Twas Mulga Bill, from Eaglehawk, that sought his own abode,
That perched above the Dead Man's Creek, beside the mountain road.
He turned the cycle down the hill and mounted for the fray,
But ere he'd gone a dozen yards it bolted clean away.
It left the track, and through the trees, just like a silver streak,
It whistled down the awful slope towards the Dead Man's Creek.

It shaved a stump by half an inch, it dodged a big white-box:
The very wallaroos in fright went scrambling up the rocks,
The wombats hiding in their caves dug deeper underground,
As Mulga Bill, as white as chalk, sat tight to every bound.
It struck a stone and gave a spring that cleared a fallen tree,
It raced beside a precipice as close as close could be;
And then as Mulga Bill let out one last despairing shriek
It made a leap of twenty feet into the Dead Man's Creek.

'Twas Mulga Bill, from Eaglehawk, that slowly swam ashore:
He said, ''I've had some narrer shaves and lively rides before;
I've rode a wild bull round a yard to win a five-pound bet,
But this was the most awful ride that I've encountered yet.
I'll give that two-wheeled outlaw best; it's shaken all my nerve
To feel it whistle through the air and plunge and buck and swerve.
It's safe at rest in Dead Man's Creek, we'll leave it lying still;
A horse's back is good enough henceforth for Mulga Bill.''

The Amateur Gardener

THE FIRST step in amateur gardening is to sit down and consider what good you are going to get by it. If you are only a tenant by the month, as most people are, it is obviously not much use your planting a fruit orchard or an avenue of oak trees, which will take years to come to maturity. What you want is something that will grow quickly, and will stand transplanting for when you move it would be a sin to leave behind you all the plants on which you have spent so much labour and so much patent manure. We knew a man once who was a bookmaker by trade — and a leger bookmaker at that — but he had a passion for horses and flowers, and when he "had a big win", as he occasionally did, it was his custom to have movable wooden stables built on skids put up in the yard, and to have tons of the best soil that money could buy carted into the garden of the premises which he was occupying. Then he would keep splendid horses in the stables, grow rare roses and show-bench chrysanthemums in the garden and the landlord passing by would see the garden in a blaze of colour, and would promise himself that he would raise the bookmaker's rent next quarter day. However, when the bookmaker "took the knock", as he invariably did at least twice a year, it was his pleasing custom to move without giving any notice. He would hitch two carthorses to the stables, and haul them away at night. He would dig up not only the roses, trees, and chrysanthemums that he had planted, but would also cart away the soil he had brought in; in fact, he used to shift the garden bodily. He had one garden that he shifted to nearly every suburb in Sydney in turn, and he always argued that change of air was invaluable for chrysanthemums. Be this as it may, the proposition is self-evident that the would-be amateur gardener should grow flowers not for posterity, nor for his landlord, nor for his creditors, but for himself.

Being determined then to go in for gardening on commonsense principles, and having decided on the class of shrubs that you mean to grow, the next thing is to consider what sort of a chance you have of growing them. If your neighbour keeps game fowls it may be taken for granted that before long they will pay you a visit, and you will see the rooster scratching your pot plants out by the roots as if they were so much straw, just to make a nice place to lie down and fluff the dust over himself. Goats will also stray in from the street, and bite the young shoots off, selecting the most valuable plants with a discrimination that would do credit to a professional gardener; and whatever valuable plant a goat bites is doomed. It is therefore useless thinking of growing any delicate or squeamish plants. Most amateur gardeners maintain a lifelong struggle against the devices of Nature, and when the forces of man and the forces of Nature come into conflict Nature will win every time. Nature has decreed that certain plants shall be hardy, and therefore suitable to suburban amateur gardens, but the suburban amateur gardener persists in trying to grow quite other plants, and in despising those marked out by Nature for his use. It is to correct this tendency that this article is written.

The greatest standby to the amateur gardener should undoubtedly be the blue-flowered shrub known as plumbago. This homely but hardy plant will grow anywhere. It naturally prefers a good soil and a sufficient rainfall, but if need be it will worry along without either. Fowls cannot scratch it up, and even a goat turns away dismayed from its hard-featured branches. The flower is not strikingly beautiful nor ravishingly scented, but it flowers nine months out of the year, and though smothered with street dust and scorched by the summer sun you will find that faithful old plumbago plugging along undismayed. A plant like this should be encouraged and made much of, but the misguided amateur gardener as a rule despises it. The plant known as the churchyard geranium is also one marked out by Providence for the amateur, as is also cosmea, a plant that comes up year after year when once planted. In creepers, bignonia and lantana will hold their own under difficulties perhaps as well as any that can be found. In trees, the Port Jackson fig is a patriotic plant to grow, and it is a fine plant to provide exercise, as it sheds its leaves unsparingly, and requires to have the whole garden swept up every day. Your aim as a student of Nature should be to encourage the survival of the fittest. In grasses, too, the same principle holds good. There is a grass called nut grass, and another called Parramatta grass, either of which will hold its own against anything living or dead. The average gardening manual gives you recipes for destroying these grasses. Why should you destroy them in favour of a sickly plant that needs constant attention? No. The Parramatta grass is the selected of Nature, and who are you to interfere with Nature?

Having thus decided to go in for strong, simple plants that will hold their own, and a bit over, you must get your implements of husbandry. A spade is the first thing, but the average ironmonger will show you an unwieldy weapon only meant to be used by navvies. Don't buy it. Get a small spade, about half-size — it is nice and light and doesn't tire the wrist, and with it you can make a good display of enthusiasm, and earn the hypocritical admiration of your wife. After digging for half an hour or so, you can get her to rub your back with any of the backache cures advertised in this journal and from that moment you will have no further need for the spade.

Besides a spade, a barrow is about the only other thing needed, and anyhow it is almost a necessity for removing cases of whisky into the house. A rake is useful sometimes as a weapon, when your terrier dog has bailed up a cat, and will not attack it till the cat is made to run. And talking of terrier dogs, an acquaintance of ours has a dog that does all his gardening. The dog is a small elderly terrier, whose memory is failing somewhat, so as soon as the terrier has planted a bone in the garden the owner slips over and digs it up and takes it away. When the terrier goes back and finds the bone gone, he distrusts his own memory, and begins to think that perhaps he has made a mistake, and has dug in the wrong place; so he sets to work and digs patiently all over the garden, turning over acres of soil in his search for the missing bone. Meanwhile, the man saves himself a lot of backache.

The sensible amateur gardener, then, will not attempt to fight with Nature but will fall in with her views. What more pleasant than to get out of bed at 11.30 on a Sunday morning, and look out of your window at a lawn waving with the feathery plumes of Parramatta grass, and to see beyond it the churchyard or stinking geranium flourishing side by side with the plumbago and the Port Jackson fig? The garden gate blows open, and the local commando of goats, headed by an aged and fragrant patriarch (locally known as De Wet from the impossibility of capturing him), rush in; but their teeth will barely bite through the wiry stalks of the Parramatta grass, and the plumbago and the fig tree fail to attract them; and before long they scale the fence by standing on one another's shoulders, and disappear into the next-door garden, where a fanatic is trying to grow show roses. After the last goat has scaled your neighbour's fence, and only De Wet is left in your garden, your little dog discovers him, and De Wet beats a hurried retreat, apparently at full speed, with the little dog exactly one foot behind him in frantic pursuit. We say apparently at full speed, because old experience has taught that De Wet can run as fast as a greyhound when he likes; but he never exerts himself to go any faster than is necessary to just keep in front of whatever dog is after him; in fact, De Wet once did run for about a hundred yards with a greyhound after him, and then he suddenly turned and butted the greyhound cranksided, as Uncle Remus would say. Hearing the scrimmage, your neighbour comes onto his verandah, and sees the chase going down the street. "Ha! that wretched old De Wet again!" he says. "Small hope your dog has of catching him! Why don't you get a garden gate like mine, so as he won't get in?" "No; he can't get in at your gate," is the reply, "but I think his commando are in your back garden now." The next thing is a frantic rush by your neighbour, falling downstairs in his haste, and the sudden reappearance of the commando skipping easily back over the fence, and through your gate into the street again, stopping to bite some priceless pot plants of your neighbour's as they come out. A horse gets in, but his hoofs make no impression on the firm turf of the Parramatta grass, and you get quite a hearty laugh by dropping a chair on him out of the first floor window, and seeing him go tearing down the street. The game fowls of your other neighbour come fluttering into your garden, and scratch and chuckle and fluff themselves under your plumbago bush; but you don't worry. Why should you? They can't hurt it: and besides, you know well enough that the small black hen and the big yellow hen, who have disappeared from the throng, are even now laying their daily eggs for you at the back of the thickest bush. Your little dog rushes frantically up and down the front bed of your garden barking and racing, and tearing up the ground, because his rival little dog who lives down the street is going past with his master, and each pretends that he wants to be at the other — as they have pretended every day for the past three years. But the performance he goes through in the garden doesn't disturb you. Why should it? By following the directions in this article you have selected plants that he cannot hurt. After breakfasting at 12 noon, you stroll out, and, perhaps, smooth with your foot or with your small spade, the inequalities made by the hens; you gather up casually the eggs that they have laid; you whistle to your little dog, and go out for a stroll with a light heart. That is the true way to enjoy amateur gardening.

Shearing with a Hoe

The track that led to Carmody's is choked and overgrown,
   The suckers of the stringybark have made the place their own;
The mountain rains have cut the track that once we used to know
When first we rode to Carmody's, a score of years ago.

The shearing shed at Carmody's was slab and stringybark,
The press was just a lever beam, invented in the Ark;
But Mrs Carmody was cook — and shearers' hearts would glow
With praise of grub at Carmody's, a score of years ago.

At shearing time no penners-up would curse their fate and weep,
For Fragrant Fred — the billy-goat — was trained to lead the sheep;
And racing down the rattling chutes the bleating mob would go
Behind their horned man from Cook's, a score of years ago.

An owner of the olden time, his patriarchal shed
Was innocent of all machines or gadgets overhead:
And pieces, locks and super-fleece together used to go
To fill the bales at Carmody's, a score of years ago.

A ringer from the western sheds, whose fame was wide and deep,
Was asked to take a vacant pen and shear a thousand sheep.
"Of course, we've only got the blades!" "Well, what I want to know:
Why don't you get a bloke to take it off 'em with a hoe?"

The Oracle at the Theatre

"Plays," said the Oracle to the Thin Man (as they sat in the third row of the gallery, waiting for the curtain to rise for the due performance of that popular melodrama *The Glazier's Revenge, or The Bloodstained Putty Knife*), "plays are not as good as they used to be."

"No," said the Thin Man.

"Actors are not as good as they used to be."

"Certainly not," said the Thin Man.

"Scenery is not as good as it used to be."

"You're right again," said the Thin Man. "Nothing is as good as it used to be; in fact, nothing ever was as good as it used to be!"

"What?" said the Oracle.

"Nothing ever was as good as it used to be," repeated the Thin Man.

"Are you trying to be sarcastic?" asked the Oracle. "If you are, I advise you to abandon the idea, because sarcasm is unsuitable coming from persons of your complexion."

"What's the matter with my complexion?"

"It's your nose," said the Oracle. "It is such a very red nose that you should not draw attention to it by trying to be sarcastic at other people's expense. Persons whose noses shine like the starboard light of an Orient steamer entering Port Jackson at midnight when there is no moon cannot afford to be disagreeably jocular in respect to the peculiar personal attributes of others."

As the orchestra finished the overture, and the drop scene rose (it is called the "drop scene" because every time it is let down between the acts the male portion of the audience goes out to have a "drop", and comes back chewing cloves and coffee beans), the two friends observed immediately in front of them a lady wearing a hat the size and shape of a wash basket. Unfortunately, she was a short lady with scarcely any neck. If her neck had been long enough to carry her hat a couple of yards nearer to the ceiling, it would not have been in the way; but then, of course, she wouldn't have worn it.

"We won't be able to see anything for that hat," grumbled the Thin Man.

"You keep calm for a second and watch me," said the Oracle. "I'll soon make her take that hat off," and he immediately put on his own hat, and sat bolt upright.

"Take that hat off! Take yer rat off! Give us a chance ter see a bit o' the stage!" and similar cries came from the people behind.

The Oracle removed his hat; so did the lady!

"I knew that would fetch her," said the Oracle to his friend; "it is an old London dodge. She naturally thought the crowd behind were singing out at her. Now we shall be able to see something of the show."

The first scene of Act One showed the interior of a poorly furnished room in Soho. Enter fair-haired young man with long legs, who begins thus:

"What would my landlady say if she but knew that I, known here as Jim the Glazier, am really nephew to the Earl of Cucumberland; that I am the Honourable Eric Trehowmuch; and that only one life prevents me becoming Viscount Purplebeak and heir to the earldom? Ha! And what would the lovely Lady Ermyntrude Plantagenet, only daughter of the Duke of Wollongong, say, did she but know that I, Eric Trehowmuch, am masquerading as a journeyman painter and glazier of Frith Street, Soho? Yet even now must I, the possible heir of 20 earls, prepare the putty for the day's work! As the immortal bard says, ' 'Tis true 'tis putty, and putty 'tis, 'tis true!' " (Slow music.)

"Is he the villain or the hero?" whispered the Thin Man.

"The hero, of course," said the Oracle. "Why do you ask such foolish questions? Can't you see his hair is fair and wavy? Heroes always have fair, wavy hair. In melodrama the villain always has very dark hair, heavy black eyebrows, and black moustache; the hero has blue eyes and fair, wavy hair."

"Ain't there any heroes in Japan?" asked the Thin Man.

"Of course there are," said the Oracle. "Why don't you read the cables about the war?"

"Well," said the Thin Man, "I never saw a Japanese with fair, wavy hair and blue eyes."

"We're not talking about Japan," replied the Oracle, irritably; "we're talking about melodrama."

"Oh, close your 'tater traps down there!" called a gentleman, in a back seat, with the charming politeness for which occupants of the gallery are universally remarkable.

"Must be a cranky-tempered chap, that," murmured the Thin Man.

"Not at all," whispered the Oracle. "This isn't the dress circle. People come to the gallery to listen to the play. If they want to chatter and jabber all the time, same as they do in the drawing-room, after worrying some reluctant vocalist to sing, they go into the dress circle with the deadheads."

"The deadheads?"

"Yes; the dramatic critics of the papers, who come on business and would far sooner be somewhere else playing billiards, and the other people who get in on the nod; they're all bundled into the dress circle in Sydney theatres."

"But," said the Thin Man, "the price of a seat is much more there."

"Of course it is," said the Oracle, "but it's always half-empty, except when there's something very special on. That's why they draft all the pressmen and deadheads into it. Everybody pays in the gallery; that's why the manager takes so much notice of the gallery's opinion. It isn't that the gallery has more brains than the dress circle, but its opinion is honest. It doesn't applaud what it doesn't like; it feels under no obligation to clap its hands when a play is absurd; it sometimes hisses the villain because he is a good actor, but it always ends with a cheer when he is called before the curtain. The gallery crowd doesn't pay much individually, but there is a lot of them, and they all pay. Their opinion settles the fate of any play. When Mr Haddon Chambers, of this township, went to London with a play called *Captain Swift*, Mr Beerbohm Tree offered to stage it at a matinee as a trial. 'If the gallery likes it, I'll take it,' said Mr Tree. The gallery did like it and Mr Chambers jumped from being a Sydney newspaper reporter to be a front-rank London playwright. Sometimes an actor will lose his temper when the gallery hisses, but it only hisses the villain as a rule, which is a compliment to the actor in the part. It is when the gallery hisses the play that actors of mediocre ability lose their tempers; but whether they do or do not, the gallery is nearly always right, and even if it isn't right its opinion is the honest public opinion of any show, from a problem play to a skipping rope dance. And it won't stand any inversion of moral principles; it must have virtue triumphant, and vice and crime duly punished. It is the opinion of the gallery that has made many problem plays a dead loss, despite the efforts of able managers and famous artists. Of course there are people in other parts of the house who belong to the same class as the folks in the gallery, only they are a bit better off, and can afford a bit better seat, but they are mixed up with others, and —"

"Shut up!" called the man behind, as the drop scene went up again.

"Certainly," said the Oracle. "We seem to have a descendant of the celebrated Earl of Chesterfield in the gallery this evening."

In the second act, the two lives that stood between the glazier and the earldom of Cucumberland were skilfully removed, in accordance with the ancient traditions of melodramatic art. They were not blown up and exploded in a motor car, as they might have been, if Mr Bland Holt or some other up-to-date manager had been in charge — their bodies were found stabbed, and beside the bodies was found a putty knife, bearing on the handle the name and address of a glazier in Frith Street, Soho!

In Act Three the hero was tried, found guilty, sentenced to death, and released under the First Offenders Act; and solemnly declared his innocence, which nobody believed, except Lady Ermyntrude.

In Act Four, Lady Ermyntrude takes the role of a female edition of Sherlock Holmes and, dressed in male attire, she haunts the neighbourhood of Frith Street, Soho, and discovers, by the fingerprint system of identification, invented by Pudd'n'head Wilson, that the double murder was really committed by a Russian Nihilist, named Blowmenozoff, who stole the putty knife to commit the murders, in order to throw suspicion on the hero. This momentous discovery was greeted with loud applause.

"I don't see," said the Thin Man, as he and the Oracle wended their way out to the nearest bar, to see what time it was, "I don't see why that Russian cove wanted to kill 'em."

"Did it for practice," said the Oracle.

"Practice?" queried the Thin Man.

"Certainly," said the Oracle. "They're always trying to find a way to kill the Czar, and this is a new idea. A window gets broken in the Winter Palace, and the glazier, a Nihilist in disguise, comes to put in a new pane. The Czar looks in to see how it is being done, and is stabbed with the putty knife! Of course, the Nihilist would have to practise on somebody else before he tackled the Czar, for fear he made a mess of it."

"I see," said the Thin Man. "Shall we go back?"

"If you like," said the Oracle, "but there's no need. In the last act the glazier is acknowledged as the rightful Earl of Cucumberland, marries the Lady Ermyntrude amid general rejoicing, and they decide, in view of the dreadful disclosures about the declining birth rate, to raise a considerable family, and live happy ever afterwards!"

The Uplift

When the drays are bogged and sinking, then it's no use sitting
    thinking,
      You must put the teams together and must double-bank the pull.
When the crop is light and weedy, or the fleece is burred and seedy,
  Then the next year's crop and fleeces may repay you to the full.

    So it's lift her, Johnny, lift her,
    Put your back in it and shift her,
While the jabber, jabber, jabber of the politicians flows.
    If your nag's too poor to travel
    Then get down and scratch the gravel
For you'll get there if you walk it — if you don't, you'll feed the crows.

Shall we waste our time debating with a grand young country waiting
  For the plough and for the harrow and the lucerne and the maize?
For it's work alone will save us in the land that fortune gave us
  There's no crop but what we'll grow it; there's no stock but what
    we'll raise.

    When the team is bogged and sinking
    Then it's no use sitting thinking.
There's a roadway up the mountain that the old black leader knows:
    So it's lift her, Johnny, lift her,
    Put your back in it and shift her,
Take a lesson from the bullock — he goes slowly, but he goes!

My Various Schools

IN WRITING about schools which I have at different periods attended, I will pass over my infantile experience of an old dame's school in a suburb of Sydney; also of a small public school to which I crept unwillingly, like a snail, for a few months. I pass these over because I don't remember much about them, and what little I do remember is unpleasant.

The first school which I attended in the capacity of a reasoning human creature was a public school in a tired little township away out in the bush, at the back of the Never Never, if you know where that is. I lived on a station four miles from the school, and had to go up paddock every morning on foot, catch my pony, and ride him down to the house barebacked, get breakfast, ride the four miles, and be in school by half-past nine o'clock. Many a time in the warm summer mornings have I seen the wonderful glories of a bush sunrise, when comes

> The still silent change,
> When all fire-flushed the forest trees redden
> On slopes of the range,
> When the gnarl'd, knotted trunks Eucalyptian
> Seem carved, like weird columns Egyptian,
> With curious device, quaint inscription,
> And hieroglyph strange.

I think Australian boys who have never been at school in the bush have lost something for which town life can never compensate. However, let me get on to the school, where I mingled with the bush youngsters who, from huts and selections and homesteads far and near, had gathered there. They were a curious lot. Perhaps their most striking characteristic was their absolute want of originality. They had one standard excuse whenever they were late: "Father sent me after 'orses". They didn't garnish it with a "Sir", or anything of the sort, but day after day every boy that was late handed in the same unvarnished statement, and took his caning as a matter of course. As their parents were largely engaged in looking after horses, mostly other people's, it had colour of probability at first, but after a time it wore out and they were too lazy or too stupid to invent anything to replace it. I thought I could mend this state of things, having a particularly vigorous and cultivated imagination, so one day, when a lot were late, I supplied each of them with a different excuse. One was to have forgotten his book and gone back for it, another was to have been misled as to the time by the sun getting up unusually late (not one in fifty had a clock in their house), another was to have been sent on an errand to the storekeeper's and been delayed by the clerk, and so forth. I was privileged and licensed to be late myself, having so far to come, so I simply walked in hurriedly as though I had done my best to arrive early and went to my seat. Then came the first of my confederates. "What makes you late, Ryan?" Ryan gasped, his eyes rolled, his jaw dropped, and then out it came, the old familiar formula — "Father sent me after 'orses." It was second nature to the boy. And all the others, one by one, as they faced the music, brought out the same old story, and took two cuts of the cane on each hand as per usual. I gave them up after that; my inventive talent was wasted upon such people.

The visit of the inspector used to be a great event in the school. Theoretically the inspector was supposed to come unheralded, and to drop on the master promiscuous-like, and so catch the school unprepared; but practically, when the inspector was in the town, the master always had a boy stationed on the fence to give warning of his approach, and by the time the inspector had toiled up the long hill to the school, that boy was back in his seat and every youngster was studying for dear life; and when the inspector asked us questions in arithmetic, the master used to walk absent-mindedly behind him and hold up his fingers to indicate the correct answer. Oh, he was a nice pedagogue!

In writing of a school, one ought to say something about the lessons, but I remember absolutely nothing of the curriculum, except the "handers" which formed, for the boys at any rate, the one absorbing interest of each day.

"Handers" were blows on the palm of the hand, administered with a stout cane. They were dealt out on a regular scale, according to the offence; not being able to answer a question, one on each hand; late at school, two on each hand; telling lies, three on each hand, etc., etc. The school was in a very cold climate, and perhaps the "handers" didn't sting at all on a cold frosty morning! Oh no, not in the least. We used to have wild theories that if you put resin on the palm of your hand the cane would split into a thousand pieces and cut the master's hand severely, but none of us had ever seen resin, so one's dreams of revenge were never realised. Sometimes fierce, snorting old Irishwomen used to come to the school and give the master some first-class Billingsgate for having laid on the "handers" too forcibly or too frequently on the hardened palm of her particular Patsy or Denny. We used to sit with open mouths and bulging eyes, while the dreaded pedagogue cowered before the shrill and fluent abuse of these ladies. They always had the last word, in fact the last hundred or more words, as their threats and taunts used to be distinctly audible as they faded away down the dusty hill.

When the railway came to the town, the children of the navvies came to the school, and how they did wake it up! Sharp, cunning little imps, they had travelled and shifted about all over the colony, they had devices for getting out of "handers" such as we had never dreamt of, they had a fluency in excuse and a fertility in falsehood which we could admire but never emulate. Sometimes their parents the navvies used to go on prolonged drinking bouts, and contract a disease, known to science, I believe, as "delirium tremens", but in our vocabulary as "the horrors" or "the jumps". The townsfolk shortened up even this brief nomenclature — they used simply to say that so-and-so "had 'em" or "had got 'em". Well do I remember the policeman, a little spitfire of a man about five feet nothing, coming to the school and stating that a huge navvy named Cornish Jack had "got 'em", and was wandering about the town with them, and he called upon the schoolmaster in the Queen's name to come and assist him to arrest "Cornish Jack". The teacher did not like the job at all, and his wife abused the policeman heartily, but it ended in the whole school going, and we marched through the town till we discovered the quarry seated on a log, pawing the air with his hands. The sergeant and the teacher surrounded him, so to speak, but to our disgust he submitted very quietly and was bundled into a cart and driven off to the lock-up. Such incidents as these formed breaks in the monotony of school life and helped to enlarge our knowledge of human nature.

There was not wanting some occasional element of sadness too. I remember one day all the boys were playing at the foot of a long hill covered with fallen timber; it was after school hours and one of the boys was given a bridle by his father and told to catch a horse that was feeding in hobbles on the top of the hill and bring him down. The boy departed, nothing loath, and caught the animal, a young half-broken colt, and boy-like mounted him barebacked and started to ride him down. The colt ran away with him and came sweeping down the hill at a racing pace, jumping fallen logs and stones, and getting faster and faster every moment. The boy rode him well, but at length he raced straight at a huge log, and suddenly, instead of jumping it, swerved off, throwing the boy with terrific force among the big limbs. His head was crushed in and he was dead before we got up to him. His people were Irish folk and the intense, bitter sadness of their grief was something terrible.

I left the bush school soon after that, and went to a private school in the suburbs of Sydney: a nice quiet institution where we were all young gentlemen, and had to wear good clothes instead of hobnailed boots and moleskins in which my late schoolmates invariably appeared. Also we were ruled by moral suasion instead of "handers"; a thing that I appreciated highly.

Very little of interest occurred there; a sickening round of lessons and washing. Nobody ever "had 'em", nobody was ever sent after horses; nobody wore spurs in school; most of the boys learnt dancing and some could play the piano. Let us draw a veil over it, and hurry on to the grammar school.

I remember, in form 3A, that two of us, who sat in the second row from the back, established a vendetta against two boys who sat in the second row from the front. We used to make single-handed excursions against them in the following manner. While the master was writing on the blackboard and had his back turned to the class, one of us would glide silently out of the seat, drop on all fours and crawl round the desks up behind the unsuspecting foe. Then for a brief and glorious instant he would rear himself up behind them, hit each of them an awful blow on the head with his open hand, of course making as little noise as possible, and then glide back as silently as he came. They used to do the same thing to us whenever they got the chance, but, sitting as they did in front of us, it was very rarely that either of them could manage to drop out of the seat without us noticing. Sometimes they managed it when we were talking, which was often enough, goodness knows, and then they stalked on us like red Indians are supposed to do, and the first we knew of it was an awful thud on the head, and a smothered chuckle from the enemy. Of course this was great for the rest of the class, and they used to watch the stalking with keen interest. I remember one fatal day that my comrade, having stalked his quarry in a masterly manner, hit them each such a spank that our form master heard the thud and looked around. He found all the boys on the broad grin; and all looking at one particular part of the room, where in fact my partner was crouched, hiding behind two other boys. The master sternly inquired what was going on, got no answer, hesitated a moment, and then came down. There on all fours under the desk was this boy. "What are you doing here?" "Nothing, sir." "What is your object? What did you come for? Why are you grovelling about on the floor instead of being in your seat?" "I don't know, sir." "You must have had some reason for coming here?" "No, sir." The master gave it up in despair. He didn't even punish the boy. It was a dark and inexplicable mystery to him, and he left it alone. He thought it was some form of religious observance, perhaps. Anyhow I wouldn't advise the present generation to try it on.

My Various Schools

"What is your object! What did you come for! Why are you grovelling about on the floor instead of being in your seat?"